Demons are Real

By Joy Vassal

Copyright © 2006 by Joy Vassal

Demons are Real
by Joy Vassal

Printed in the United States of America

ISBN 1-60034-056-3

All rights reserved solely by the author. The author guarantees all contents are original and do not infringe upon the legal rights of any other person or work. No part of this book may be reproduced in any form without the permission of the author. The views expressed in this book are not necessarily those of the publisher.

Unless otherwise indicated, Bible quotations are taken from King James Version. Copyright © 1984 year 1977 by Thomas Nelson Inc. Publishers, Nashville.

www.xulonpress.com

Foreword

We are living in a time when many North American pastors, teachers, and theologians have chosen to sanitize the gospel in order to present a more tolerable message for the 21st century church. They preach a gospel of blessings and prosperity while many Christians and people of the world are terrorized and traumatized by demons. Like Ezekiel the prophet to Israel, God has called prophetess Joy Vassal, to remind the church that we are still, and constantly, involved in spiritual warfare. Through her own personal testimony and research on demonology, the Rev. Vassal proves unequivocally that "Demons are Real."

Many church pastors, leaders, and theologians are reluctant to preach or teach about demons, which render their churches, parishes, and seminaries vulnerable to the maladies of this evil culture. Rev. Vassal, on the other hand, has faced the topic with tenacity and courage in order to warn her readers and arm them against the influence of the wicked one. Researching and writing about this subject was a bold feat indeed since she had not only seen these powers at work in the lives of those around her, she had witnessed, experienced and overcome the working of demons in her own life.

Aside from those who are uncomfortable with teaching or preaching about this study, many do not even believe in the demonic. Instead, they attribute demonic problems and events to be a result of mental, emotional, physical, or psychological problem. As a matter of fact, I have sat in seminary classes where professors taught that many of the demonic cases the Bible claims Jesus handled were merely His healing of emotional and mental disorders. That is one of the major problems of our times. Because of the growth in education and knowledge there are many who would choose to eradicate a biblical truth for science and psychology. Those who truly read the Bible must conclude that if there is a heaven and a hell then there must be angels, ministering servants for the saints of God, and demons, the servant of Satan. Reading this book will help you understand the power of demons, but more importantly, you will recognize the awesome power of God, in the child of God, over the power of evil in our world.

Joy has shared, from her personal experience and the testimony of her mother and other Christians, proof that the demonic realm is still real today. She has taken time to outline various designations for demons and devils. She has made it clear that demons are personalities without bodies - inhuman but functioning in humans. She confirms beyond a shadow of a doubt that demons are powerful, but provides us with the weapons to conquer demonic power through our all-powerful God.

Joy illustrates how many Christians unknowingly invite evil spirit into their homes through certain artifacts and souvenirs they have collected. She clearly shows that many Christian homes have experienced darkness, trouble, and sicknesses because of these strange intruders. She further shares that when it was discovered that these artifacts or souvenirs were the reasons for their problems and they were removed, peace, healing, and tranquility returned.

Reading this book will help you to understand the steps leading to possession and how to be set free. Rev. Vassal closes by showing readers that they have the power, in the word of God, to live a life victorious over Satan, and demons. Knowing about the power of the demonic world and its limitations, in comparison to the Kingdom of God, will give you a greater appreciation for the gift of God to you - Salvation.

Daniel J. Vassell Sr.
Cross Cultural Youth/Singles Ministries Coordinator & author of best selling book, The Love Factor in Marriage.

Acknowledgments

It is with great delight I give credence to the King, Eternal, immortal, invisible, the only wise God. Awesome is this supernatural being who dwells in unapproachable light, which we have never, nor will ever see. We believe that He reigns for evermore.

I Would like to express my sincere gratitude and appreciation to the following individuals who have contributed tremendously to the success of this book. Their patience, support, suggestions, consultation and relentless work will never be forgotten.

First, I would like to thank Bishop, Doctor Huel Wilson and Mrs. Wilson for their leadership at the West Toronto New Testament Church of God. Their love, encouragement and prayers are much appreciated.

I would like to thank the Administrative Bishop Andrew Binda for his prayers and reviewing of my manuscript.

I would like to thank Bishop Daniel Vassell (my cousin and the author of Love Factor) for also reviewing my manuscript and his encouragement to make this great work a reference book.

I would like to thank Reverend Colin Esseboom for his enthusiasm and encouragement to go forward and edify the body of Christ.

This book could never have come into being without the relentless work of Judy Simpson. She read, typed, reviewed and edited this manuscript for three years.

Thanks to Xulon Press for editoral and copyediting services.

Clairmount Humphrey (founder for GM Radio 2CP- was very helpful when he prayed and recommended the Xulon Press Inc.

God allowed these wonderful anointed men and women of his choice to contribute to the success of this book. Pastor Everton Powell, Pastor Jeffery Anderson, Richard Saunders, Bishop Rupert Bourne, Pastor Andrew Akinzuyi, Reverend Angela Solomon, Father Bill Lammie, Laurel Falconer, Julian Francis, Daserita Lawson, Albert Hall, Marjorie Mullings and Glenda Roye Hamilton.

Let me not hesitate to mention my two beautiful daughters, Lenesha and Sheree and the best mom in the world, Mrs. Beryl Vassell, for their undying love and devotion.

God has indeed orchestrated every step of this great work so I give him thanks for all things for it is the will of God in Christ Jesus. I pray that God will give you all the spirit of wisdom and revelation that you may know him better and I pray that the eyes of your understanding will be enlightened that you may not be ignorant of the devil's wiles.

Dedication

Mrs. Beryl Vassell (*Mother*)

Lenesha and Sheree (*Daughters*)

Table of Contents

Introduction		xi
Chapter 1:	Bitter Weed	13
Chapter 2:	Putting Demons to Flight	19
Chapter 3:	Witch	27
Chapter 4:	Leaving Home	33
Chapter 5:	Dealing with the Demonic	41
Chapter 6:	Dealing with Witchcraft	55
Chapter 7:	God's Eccentrics	65
Chapter 8:	Confounding the "Wise"	73
Chapter 9:	Evidences of the Demonic	81
Chapter 10:	Demonic Possession	87
Chapter 11:	Demons and Disease	99
Chapter 12:	Are We Ready?	109
Epilogue		115

Introduction

> Wisdom is a principal thing; therefore get wisdom: and with all thy getting get understanding.
>
> Proverbs 4:7

In these last days, it is imperative that ones' understanding is enlightened regarding the evil forces of darkness that pervade the Scriptures, from Genesis to Revelation. It is no myth or fairytale that evil forces of darkness contends or fight against humanity. Neither the devil nor the principalities, powers, rulers of the darkness of this world and spiritual wickedness in high places are figments of our imagination.

The first war to be recorded in the scriptures was initiated by the devil after pride entered his heart and he desired equality with God. He was then transformed and excommunicated from the prestigious position of guarding the throne of God and being a music leader in heaven. This war was evidently between Satan and his angels, and Michael and his angels. Michael won the battle because he served God, and the King of Glory, strong and mighty, has never lost a battle. Angry with God because of his fallen position, Satan entered into the Garden of Delight and caused the first upheaval among mankind—the first sin.

It's evident that the devil is an intelligent and wise being. He did not choose Adam to tempt; instead, he approached Eve, the weaker vessel who was limited in knowledge and experience. Eve succumbed to his wiles and Adam sided with her; therefore, as the Word of the Lord declares, all who followed Adam and Eve have sinned and come short of the glory of God.

The devil prowls around seeking whom he may devour. He is busy going to and fro seeking to kill, steal and destroy humanity. He delights in binding people with emotional, mental and even physical chains. One woman was bound by the devil for 18 years, but Jesus loosened her chains. The Bible also tells of a man who was possessed by 6,000 devils, but Jesus cast them out and the man was delivered.

The devil causes physical maladies and catastrophes in people's lives. But it doesn't matter what you are going through—Jesus is able to set you free. Jesus spoiled all principalities and powers; He openly made a show of them, triumphing over them all.

We have a right as His children to use His name and His Word to pull down and smash to pieces every one of the devil's plans. Let this be an encouragement to you that we are more than conquerors through faith in Jesus Christ.

CHAPTER 1

Bitter Weed

The heart is deceitful above all things, and desperately wicked: who can know it?

Jeremiah 17:9

I grew up in a small community in a remote area in the parish of Manchester Jamaica. My family consisted of my mother and father; one sister, four brothers, and me. With a population of 1,500 people, This small community was sometimes referred to as Small Garden and Bitter Weed (an expression denoting the craftiness of its inhabitants). The town was in a mountainous area where much of the land was cultivated. Many people of this community migrated to foreign countries to make a better life while others pursued skills and trades appropriate for their lives in Jamaica. The general attitude of the people, however, made it very difficult for the people to make very much of themselves; even those who were ambitious often didn't succeed. Some tried to improve themselves or learn new things but didn't follow through because there was no one or nothing to encourage them.

The majority of residents of Bitter Weed had encountered the demonic. It was common to hear people talking about duppies or ghosts, Obeah, Voodoo, black magic, mother woman and witchcraft. People often mentioned the unexplained disappearance of personal belongings. Some didn't like attending school, others didn't have the desire to work, while some had terrible sores that never healed.

Some people would run off the road because of a phenomenon known as "rolling calf." Rolling calf is believed to be an invisible entity that makes such a frightening noise that the adrenaline in your body causes you to run for your life. In addition, stones often rained down on peoples' homes, but the cause of all this mischief was a power that cannot be seen.

The Word of the Lord declares that the heart is deceitful above all things and desperately wicked. If you entertain wickedness in your heart, the desire to kill and destroy people may well be carried out.

> And he saith unto them, Are ye so without understanding also? Do ye not perceive, that whatsoever thing from without entereth into the man, it cannot defile him; because it entereth not into his heart, but into the belly, and goeth out into the draught, purging all meats? And he said, that which cometh out of the man, that defileth the man. For from within, out of the heart of men, proceed evil thoughts, adulteries, fornications, murders, thefts, covetousness, wickedness, deceit, lasciviousness, an evil eye, blasphemy, pride, foolishness: All these evil things come from within, and defile the man.
>
> Mark 7:18-23

Many people who lived in our area seemed predisposed to bringing about the horrible demise of their neighbors and friends. Evil was in their hearts at all times. It was a way of life where I grew up. These people spent many sleepless nights, plotting and scheming to overthrow and control others, and they had absolutely no remorse. Their lives were bent on the devastation and destruction of peoples' lives. They went to bed late and rose early to go out to "peep" (seek out a wizard or witch). Woe be to those who peep! Your steps are surely slippery because God shall punish you for your wicked deeds against the innocent. Psalm 91:8; says, only with thine eyes shalt thou behold and see the reward of the wicked.

These devious ones devoured their neighbors with words and deeds, not fearing the almighty God who knows about the traps and nets that they have set. I personally experienced the work of these evil people and had to flee Jamaica and leave my family behind in order to save my life.

My father was one of the blessings of my life. He was an exceptional father and a man of God. To me he is second only to the Almighty One, the Holy One of Israel. A lovable, incomparable father and a fine soldier of the cross of Jesus Christ, my father was a strict disciplinarian who lived a godly life.

He established this same standard for his family. He knew where he could find help and mercy, and he never lay down at night or arose in the morning without approaching the throne of grace. Prayer and fasting were two spiritual weapons he relied on to keep him sane on his pilgrim's journey.

Dad would rather go to a prayer and fasting service than attend a wedding or funeral. He knew that prayer and fasting were two weapons that would release the explosive power of the Holy Spirit to destroy the bands of wickedness, extinguish the fiery darts of the enemy and help pull down every stronghold. When my father died in the year 2000, I was devastated because I knew that the attacks of the evil one had caused him to suffer many afflictions.

It's said that behind every great man stands a great woman. That was the case with my father and mother. Like a vessel that conveys the gospel of Jesus Christ, my mother is like the dynamic Sarah of the Old Testament who called her husband lord or master.

Like Mary the mother of Jesus, who bore the Word of God in her innermost being, my mother spoke the living Word of God season after season. I mention this because we are referred to as living stones in the Word of God.

1 Peter 2:5; ye also, as lively stones, are built up a spiritual house, an holy priesthood, to offer up spiritual sacrifices, acceptable to God by Jesus Christ. She frequently visits the throne of grace and pours out her soul like the persistent Hannah of the Old Testament.

She followed the Word of the Lord, which says in Hebrews 4:16; "Let us therefore come boldly unto the throne of grace, that we may obtain mercy and find grace in the time of trouble."

A devout, pious, humble, sincere, loyal, loving and obedient woman of God, my mother holds various positions in the church she attends. She's a teacher, preacher, Superintendent, Mother of the Church, and choir member whom God has equipped well. She abounds in good works, thus glorifying the Lord. She also has the blessing and anointing to minister to people bound by Satan and his demons.

Strong and mighty in battle, the King of Glory has used her to pull down demonic strongholds in peoples' lives. Thanks be to God, He has never allowed her to lose a battle. Whenever there is evidence of demonic activity where she lives my mother is always the first to be summoned.

It's a joy to see the oppressed, depressed and suppressed set free by a faithful woman of God, especially in this time when the urgent cry is for a vessel who will go forth and free God's children from demonic strongholds. My mother's power over the demonic, however, puts those close to her in jeopardy. Nevertheless, because of her relationship with God her family has always been protected from serious harm.

When my uncle, a school principal in Mandeville who refused to give one of the teachers a raise, had a demonic invasion and was very ill, my mother was summoned. She began praying for her brother and prayed until she was able to take authority over the demon in the all-powerful Name of Jesus and the demon had to flee.

> And these signs shall follow them that believe; In my name shall they cast out devils; they shall speak with new tongues.
>
> Mark 16:17

This passage is most applicable to my mother. Demons were afraid of my mother and could not withstand the resistance she gave them. The Word of God declares in Psalm 60:12, "Through God we shall do valiantly: for He it is that shall tread down our enemies." James chapter 4:7; says, submit yourselves therefore to God. Resist the devil, and he will flee from you.

Although my parents lived an exemplary life none of their children emulated them. We would play church for a few weeks then got entangled again in the yoke of bondage. For my parents to survive as long as they did in the district where we lived, Jesus' blood was no doubt their coverage; I thank God for the protection that is in Jesus' blood. There is also authority in the incorruptible blood of Jesus and it will never lose its power.

Because of my mother, the angels of the Lord God had taken charge of us as children and protected us for some time. Eventually, however, as we got older, the time came for us to prove God's power for ourselves.

My eldest brother was a very ambitious young man. A construction worker by trade, he was very caring, looking out for Mom and Dad, brothers and his sisters. He dressed in the latest fashions and also gained people's respect as one of the best disc jockeys around. Suddenly something went dreadfully wrong. He became a demented person who didn't even groom himself properly.

He lost interest in work, swore at people, including Mom and Dad, and burped and spit frequently. He has never been the same. He lives as a vagabond who sometimes stops by for a visit. I often ask, "Lord, what went wrong? How can this happen? What happened?" I often prayed and summoned God. Vengeance is His. He will repay the wicked ones in time.

Many people asked Mom if wicked people had hurt her son. My mother said, "Yes, but God will fix it for me." How could someone with such great potential, so well respected, become the black sheep of the town? My brother's downfall is still the talk of the town. I say, "Woe be to those who practice witchcraft! Satan and his demons come to kill, steal and destroy humanity. That's why God distinctly warns those who are meddling in such wickedness. Innocent people are trapped and ensnared by such devious practices."

My sister's goals and aspirations were cut short when she became pregnant at age 15, and my two other brothers were never able to hold on to their dreams and ambitions. I was the only member of the family who attained higher learning education and was able to write the Jamaica School Certificate and General Certificate Education Examinations, of which I was successful. This qualified me to teach in a private high school in Jamaica. During this time in my life, I was very excited to know that the knowledge and education gained over the years were imparted to others in an effective manner.

CHAPTER 2

Putting Demons to Flight

When I was about 17 years old, I had my first date. My high school boyfriend came from a very brilliant family. He was a very brilliant mathematics student who had also passed various subjects in General Certificate Education Examination. This examination was one of the hardest set by the British standards. As a result, when a student was successful, one celebrates his success. He was tall, dark and handsome and he had attended two prominent high schools. He was also a very outstanding sports figure who was written up in *The Jamaica Daily Gleaner* many times. We dated for seven years, got engaged and then decided to tie the knot. We hadn't sought our parents' approval. We thought we didn't have to.

Patrick, my new husband, was a good provider and a very caring person. He worked as a clerk and supervisor at one of the Alumina Plants, a company which produces bauxite in the parish of St. Elizabeth. At age 25 I had everything I needed for my comfort. I hardly even did housework since we had a live-in housekeeper. All seemed to be going very well during the first year of our marriage but unbeknownst to me, trials and trouble were brewing. My peace of mind and comfort didn't last for long. The wholeness of my body, mind and spirit was affected for many reasons and things began to go very wrong.

At times I was so sick I couldn't explain to anyone how I felt. It was too weird. At other times I was unexplainably afraid. My condition went from bad to worse and I became weak, tired and depressed. I thought my only refuge at that time would be my doctor.

I visited him every two weeks. During the initial visits he was very polite, caring and concerned but after a few visits he totally changed and I became a nuisance to him. Finally one day he said, "Joy, I know you have health insurance but I do not need to see you every two weeks, especially when there is no diagnosis. Others will take your money but I won't. I need to speak to your husband to see if there's any possible solution to your problems." I left his office in complete despair feeling that now there was truly no hope.

My next step was to make an appointment with a Catholic priest. He listened to me but could offer no help. Shortly after that visit I got pregnant. Things hadn't changed for me. My husband, who was an excellent worker, got fired and couldn't find a job right away. I managed to pay the bills for a while but then things got really tough and I decided to move back with my parents. I told my husband to go to his parents since they didn't live far from my parents' home. He chose to stay with me, and my parents welcomed him.

Things quieted down for a while when we moved home, but everyone was watching us and asking about us. Some people laughed because they thought we had been living too luxuriously in Mandeville. Only the wicked rejoice over a person's misfortune. It wasn't long before I felt the presence of something evil around me. I didn't know what to say or do because I wasn't yet a Christian. I did not yet know that when you are a joint heir with Jesus your protection is guaranteed.

> For he shall give his angels charge over thee, to keep thee in all thy ways.
>
> Psalm 91:11

The scripture says one person may chase a thousand but two will put ten thousand to flight. But how could I have chased evil spirits when I didn't have a relationship with God? I wasn't part of the family of God. The lintels of my doorpost had no blood on them; therefore I was laid bare for the enemy to ravage.

For a while I walked from the freezer into the fiery furnace. I felt so cold at intervals during my ordeal that I thought I was placed in a refrigerator, then immediately after this weird sensation, I felt like

I was placed in an oven at 400 degrees Fahrenheit. It was a sensation of death and hell and it was terrifying. Despite my experience, I decided not to give in to the cares of life. I wanted to make something of myself. We got a loan and had some renovations done to the house, including an expansion.

Then my dad and I decided to do a little business together. We bought a few chickens and pigs, which we kept at the rear of the house. I enjoyed feeding these animals after work and found this task interesting and exciting. After obtaining excellent grades in social biology, human biology and religious knowledge, I was invited and encouraged by the principal to teach these subjects. My job, on the other hand, had become quite disappointing, embarrassing and humiliating after I slept through 15 minutes of the half an hour that I should have been teaching students on the job. Everyone knew I wasn't well. Some even thought I was pregnant. I had given birth to my first daughter Lenesha, so I was definitely not interested to get pregnant. I was totally overwhelmed by what I could not explain or understand.

One day as I was walking home my feet became so heavy they could hardly carry me. I dragged them on the ground because I had no energy. I managed to drag myself to a cousin's home. She was outside and I told her I couldn't make it home because my energy was depleted. She told me, rather harshly, "You're a young girl; do you believe in God?" I barely answered "yes" under my breath. She said, "Well, let's go inside and pray."

I wasn't a Christian, but I knelt down and she began to pray. She held on to her tummy and groaned, and within less than a minute she said, "You are surrounded by demons. I cannot manage them alone. Please tell your mom to call the elders of the church." Back then it was the elders of the church who were summoned to pray for the afflicted, as directed in scripture.

> Is any among you afflicted? Let him pray. Is any merry? Let him sing songs. Is any sick among you? Let him call for the elders of the church; and let them pray for him, anointing him with oil in the name of the Lord. And the prayer of faith shall save the sick, and the Lord shall raise him up; and if

he have committed sins, they shall be forgiven him. Confess your faults one to another, and pray one for another, that he may be healed. The effectual fervent prayer of a righteous man availeth much.

James 5:13-16

I eventually became well enough to walk home. I told my mother about the situation and she spoke with the elders on my behalf asking them to come and pray. Before the elders arrived my vitality was drained away as with the fervent heat of summer. I looked pale. While others joked I just curled up and slept. My friends who had come from next door then realized that something was dreadfully wrong.

The elders arrived to pray for me one evening after their church meeting. Their prayer was so powerful it sounded as if they had just set foot on Mount Carmel. They were speaking in tongues as the Spirit gave them utterance and they were on fire, ignited by the Holy Spirit to take authority over Satan and his demons.

One of the mothers said, "What is this old man doing in your house? I command you now in the name of Jesus to leave." My eyes popped open because I couldn't see anything. I wanted to see what they had seen. I didn't realize that demons don't have bodies and they had to be spiritually discerned. The naked eye cannot see demons but those with discernment can see the manifestation of a demon possessing a person. It's amazing, yet quite frightening, because the demon was right there with me in the kitchen and I didn't know it. How can an unbeliever discern the spiritual? The Word of the Lord tells us that we cannot see what is spiritually discerned.

But the natural man receiveth not then things of the Spirit of God; for they are foolishness unto him: Neither can he know them, because they are spiritually discerned.

1 Corinthians 2:14

One of the prayer warriors held on to my mother's tummy but she directed her to me. She laid her hands on my tummy and began to mourn. I knew something was wrong because prior to all this, I had always had burning sensations, aches and pains and yeast infections every month. I often felt something warm crawling up my legs. I dreaded that; I would look to see what it was but I always found nothing. I was often at a loss to figure out how I could make sense of this weird phenomenon.

One day I had a confrontation with a woman in my district who told me, "If I have to have sex with a monkey gal, I'm going to fix you. You're going to hold your belly and bawl." I didn't have the foggiest idea what she was talking about or what she intended to do. All I knew was that things began to make sense to me but I still didn't fully understand.

The demon assigned to me would try to destroy me but it couldn't resist the *dunamis* power that was at work in these praying mothers of the Church. *Dunamis* is a Greek word which means the "can do" power or the enabling power of the Holy Ghost. The Word of the Lord declares that the power of the Holy Spirit is greater than that of the devil and his demons.

> Ye are of God, little children, and have overcome them: Because greater is he that is in you, than he that is in the world.
>
> 1 John 4:4

God's Word says it, the mothers believed it, and they commanded this demon to take its flight. It had to go.

> And these signs shall follow them that believe; In my name shall they cast out devils and they shall speak with new tongues.
>
> Mark 16:17

There is power and authority in the name of Jesus to pull down the strongholds of Satan and his demons. 2 Corinthians 10: 4-5 for the weapons of our warfare are not carnal, but mighty through God to the pulling down of strongholds; Casting down imaginations and every high thing that exaleth itself against the knowledge of God, and bringing into captivity every thought to the obedience of Christ.

Praise God we can call upon Him, when we are in trouble, he is able to give us the victory. Psalm 91:15; says, "When they call to me, I will answer them; when they are in trouble, I will be with them. I will rescue them and honor them." God's children, who are called by His name, will certainly be protected. The enemy cannot come near us; neither can he harm us. These holy women of God hearkened into the Word of God and anointed me with oil; then they prayed and left.

The fervent prayer of a righteous man is always powerful. Why do I say this? Because James 5:16 tells us that we are to confess our faults one to another, and pray one for another, that we may be healed. The prayer of a righteous man is powerful. The demon had to flee because the Word of God tells us to submit to God and resist the devil, and he will flee from you.

The demon came back at about midnight but that was because I wasn't a child of God. I didn't have the hedge of God's protection. I was not dressed for war. I wasn't wearing the full armor of God. My head was exposed; no helmet of salvation was in place. Neither was the breastplate of righteousness in place. No truth girded my waist. I was not wearing the right kind of shoes; my feet weren't shod with the gospel of preparation of peace. I was walking on Satan's turf and my spiritual eyes were yet to be opened by receiving Jesus into my heart. The Word of God, the sword of the Spirit hadn't empowered me richly and I did not know how to pray.

When my husband came home that night he was terrified by a black cat that followed him, crying, from the time he got off the company bus until he reached my parents' home. Shortly after he came in something strange happened. After he settled down I decided to go to bed. The minute I lay down, some kind of entity overshadowed me and weighed me down.

I felt as if someone had thrown a thousand tons of bricks on me. I called out to my mother and she came immediately and began to call to our refuge and strength. The Word of God declares in Psalm 46:1, God is our refuge and strength, a very present help in trouble. And was I ever in trouble. The people who had come to pray over me told me that a demon was summoned to kill me and I couldn't even see it. Where would Satan attack me—in the eyes, or upper or lower extremities? The armor of God helps protect us from our enemies.

> The thief cometh not, but for to steal, and to kill, and to destroy.
> John 10:10

> Above all, taking the shield of faith, wherewith ye shall be able to quench all the fiery darts of the wicked.
> Ephesians 6:16

When my mother came to me and realized what was going on, she began to petition the God of her salvation. She exclaimed, "Father, I'm alone but you're in control." Before she made that statement God knew what He was going to do. If He had to raise up a stone to help contend with this demon, then He would. The Bible tells us that where one person can chase away a thousand, two people together can put ten thousand to flight.

His Word declares that before we call, He will answer. As the words left my mother's mouth I felt a surge of energy or power moving from my feet upward. It was overpowering and enlightening. Swayed by the awesome presence of God I began to walk through the house in search of my husband.

When I reached him I began to beat him with my hands. I couldn't stop myself. He was so frightened he didn't say a word, but just backed away from me, blocking the blows. After all this flogging I bowed down and began to worship God! I slept with my parents and was fine for the rest of the morning.

When I awoke my husband said I had beaten the hell out of him but I felt I ought to serve God. Was God calling me then? My aunt had said in the prayer meeting held at my home that "You're called, young lady." I didn't know what she meant. I got myself ready, went to work and had a great day. That would be the last "great day" I would have for some time.

CHAPTER 3

Visit to a Witch

When I returned home from work the day after I had assaulted My husband, I went outside to do the thing I liked doing best — feeding the chickens. As I watched the chickens eating their food, I felt something like a needle or pin penetrated my left thigh. I was frightened and exclaimed, "Jesus Christ!" I looked to see if it was an insect or maybe something else, but there was nothing there. I immediately went inside and told my family but no one got excited. We thought it was just "one of those things."

The following morning my mother went out on church errands, Dad went to the fields to tend his crops and I was home alone. When I got out of bed I realized that my left leg had swollen to five times the size of the right leg. I panicked and called out for Elizabeth, my next-door neighbor. I had what appeared to be a condition known as elephantiasis—an enlarging of the tissues, usually in a leg or arm. Elizabeth took me to her house. By then I was shaking like a reed so she covered me with a warm blanket. We waited for a member of my family to come home.

Some time passed before my dad came home. When he saw my leg he dashed out of the house. Within minutes a van pulled up at the gate and drove me to my Aunt Dorothy's house 14 miles away. When we arrived at my aunt's house they got me into bed.

I was as wild as a reindeer and the room was powerfully hot. I was totally out of control, pulling my hair out of my head, screaming and fighting like a wild bull. My aunt was very concerned and my dad, my aunt and her family gathered around me. My mother, my

Aunt Rose and some of her church friends soon arrived and began praying.

The prayers of God's righteous people are ever powerful and there is no doubt in my mind that their prayers were prayers of faith. In James 5:16, the Word of the Lord says that the effectual fervent prayer of a righteous man availeth much.

A friend of mine had previously taken me to see some kind of witch who chanted, smoked and puffed smoke onto a dark round object. I was dumbstruck as I tried to figure out what she was doing and what significance it had. At one point she cried out, "Why are they trying to kill you? Such a nice girl! What could you have done to them?" I wanted to ask who she was talking to but I remained speechless. Meanwhile she got out some bottles and poured a little ointment from each into a bath pan.

She then poured a little Jaze (a very offensive disinfectant used for animals) into the mixture and asked me to take off my clothes and get into the pan. Under my breath I muttered, "What kind of disgrace is this?" Little did I know that the reproach was going to be a public thing. After she had jazed me down, I put my clothes on and thought everything was going to be just fine.

I listened to her instructions: bathe in the liquid she'd given me and throw eggs in a certain direction before I went to bed. I then headed for home, with a silver "guard ring" she had given me. Regardless of the bathing and the ring, which was supposed to protect me from the demon, the demon came back to kill me. How much power can a silver ring have compared to demonic powers? I had no protection, power, and authority over this evil spirit who had come to destroy me.

As I got onto the bus it seemed as if the aroma of Jaze annoyed one lady and she blurted out, "Who de hell smell so? Jesus Christ!" I wanted to bury myself in that bus but there was no escape. As I moved further into the bus people were sniffing the air and talking about the smell all around me.

Crying out under my breath I said, "God please send this bus flying speedily. I need to get out of here." I got off the bus, dreading the stares. I stayed clear of people until I reached home. I had been to a witch, but an encounter with a wizard was yet to come.

Discerning the Spirit of Witchcraft

This is emotional for me even now as I write, because at the time I couldn't even remember the days of the week. As my relatives continued to pray over my enlarged leg, Aunt Rose cried out, "Witchcraft!" "What is all this about?" I wondered.

Aunt Dorothy, one of my favorite aunts, was determined not to see me die by the hands of crafty people. She spoke with her husband, a policeman, who gathered together a few men. Early in the morning my aunt, her husband, a few police officers, and my husband and I set out to a parish called Trelawney. She took me to see an Obeah man, or a wizard as it is called in the Bible.

During this time I couldn't help myself and had to be carried by two persons. Although it was awkward I had no choice. My left leg was so unattractive and swollen I wanted to be attended to as soon as I got there. I had many concerns but the main one was not to bump into anyone who knew me.

I was nervous on the way to the wizard mainly because I was brought up in a Christian home where going to such a place was forbidden. The Word of the Lord declares it an abomination to consult a wizard or a witch or to consult with familiar spirits.

Leviticus chapter 20:6; and the soul that turneth after such as have familiar spirits, and after wizards, to go a whoring after them, I will even set my face against that soul, and will cut him off from among his people.

We arrived in Trelawney around 7:30 a.m. I thought we would be first and therefore would be served in the first-come, first-served basis. To my amazement and disappointment the place was very crowded but we managed to press our way through the crowd and were led into what appeared to be a church.

As it turned out, everyone who sought help from the wizard had to worship in the church before it was their turn to see him. All the women there wore white dresses and red turbans with pencils sticking out and all were very excited worshipping their master—Satan—and his many demons.

The moderator was a middle-aged man who was not impressed with the response he was getting from the so-called congregation. He began to reprimand us saying, "If you came for deliverance, then people, you better loosen yourselves and worship." I was most disturbed and wanted to find out who must we worship.

He must have read my mind, as he watched me sitting there being non-responsive as I was really sick. I was surprised as he blurted out derogatory expressions at me as to why I was not worshipping. I can now truly say that out of the abundance of his heart he spoke. He was rather frustrated. The Word of the Lord declares that it's not what we eat that defiles us, but what comes out of our hearts.

> Do not ye yet understand that whatsoever entereth in at the mouth goeth to the belly, and it is cast out into the draught? But those things which proceedeth out of the mouth came forth from the heart; and they defileth the man." For out of the heart proceed evil thoughts, murders, adulteries, fornications, thefts, false witness, blasphemies: these are things which defile a man.
>
> Matthew 15:17-19

One of the women responded to the derogatory expression that came out of his mouth "Do not speak to God's children like this, respect is necessary." I thought, "Where on earth did they discover these clowns?"

We had to line up to meet this strange man in a room that was locked all the time. It was my turn and was I ever glad. My leg was just too heavy to wait another minute. They carried me in and as soon as he saw my husband, he lashed out at him angrily and said, "Get out of here!" Patrick must have been frightened out of his wits, because I sure was.

I mumbled under by breath that the young man happened to be my husband. Then I was anxious and wanted to ask why he had to leave but I didn't.

He turned to look at me and said, "You should be dead, but I'm going to take care of you and send you back to work in two weeks." I was anxious about that, but I was watching him like Sherlock Holmes because I wondered how he acquired his information. What was his medium? How did he access these channels?

God allowed me to visit this man so as to gain knowledge that the devil (or Satan) is quite crafty. Do not take him for granted. He's intelligent and quite knowledgeable. He knows the Word of God. He twisted God's Word to Eve and thus deceived her. He quoted the Word of God to Jesus who became the Word and dwelt among men.

The wizard, a medium of Satan, took the book of books and began to read from Psalm 55:12-14: "For it was not an enemy that reproached me; then I could have borne it: neither was it he that hated me that did magnify himself against me; then I would have hid myself from him: But it was thou, a man mine equal, my guide, and my acquaintance. We took sweet counsel together, and walked into the house of God in company."

Satan has not changed his strategy. He rebelled against the God of the heavens and he is bent on using the Word. He was a liar from the beginning and is the accuser of the brethren, appearing to be genuine. But it's just a disguise or camouflage. The Word of the Lord declares that Satan is a wolf in sheep's clothing. This Obeah man or wizard could have been killed instantly for perverting the Word. The Word of God is powerful and unchangeable.

> For the word of God is quick, and powerful, sharper than any two-edged sword, piercing even to dividing asunder of soul and spirit, and of joints and marrow, and is a discerner of the thoughts and intent of the heart.
> Hebrews 4:12

After the reading from the above psalm the wizard closed the Bible. My heart pumped fast. I asked myself what this was. He took a bottle of pink ointment and poured it out into a big container. "I'm going to bathe this leg for you," he said. Two people held on to me. This was the most painful experience I've ever had. I opened my mouth and bawled like an animal in great distress. People could have heard me for miles around.

After washing down my leg he mixed some kind of concoction and rubbed it all over my leg. He then gave me a few bottles of different oils and instructed me how to use them at home. I was told to throw rice and eggs outside before bedtime. A desperate person in need of help would do just about anything to get well, but what was the significance of these things? There is no help but from Jesus; He alone can destroy the works of the devil.

I was as helpless as a baby during this period but my family bathed me and cheered me on. It's important to have a loving and caring family around. I give God thanks for my Aunt Dorothy and Aunt Rose and my mom and dad, for without them I probably would not have survived.

By the second week I felt much better, so I went back to work. Things weren't the same. Something in the air was eerie. I felt out of place, but then I figured it was because I was still deeply affected by what happened.

Aunt Dorothy decided to take me to see a family doctor because he could differentiate between a medical problem and a spiritual one. He took one look at me, shook his head and said, "I've never seen nor heard of anything like this in medical history." I knew everyone could not be wrong about the demons.

My husband moved to a new apartment back in Mandeville and came to my aunt's house to take me, along with our daughters, Lenesha and Sheree, with him. Lenesha, my first daughter, was born at Hargreve's private hospital and Sheree was born at the Mandeville public hospital in the Parish of cool, cool Manchester, Mandeville. Everyone was concerned about me moving back with Patrick, but I absolutely dreaded going.

Nevertheless Lenesha, Sheree and I went back to Mandeville. Life wasn't the same. I was afraid and nervous. I walked around shaking like a reed. I didn't want to run away, but eventually that is just what I did.

CHAPTER 4

Leaving Home

I no longer felt close to Patrick. I was unable to deal with the environment I was in. I felt I had only one recourse, and that was to leave home. I wrote my aunt in England and my cousin in Canada to send me an invitation. Both sent me invitations at the same time. I decided to go to Canada because the fare was inexpensive. My uncle's friend, who lived in Kingston, made the arrangements while my husband was working the night shift, in order to keep him from finding out about my trip.

On September 23, 1989, after saying goodbye to my mom and dad, I boarded a plane in Kingston for Toronto, leaving my husband and two daughters behind knowing nothing. Only my housekeeper knew the whole plan. It was very hard for me to leave my children, since Lenesha was only five years old and Sheree was only eight months. But I knew not how to handle the situation I found myself in and I had to do what I had to do.

My cousin Hannah took me to her church and not long after I accepted the Lord as my personal savior. I needed a refuge for my soul and Jesus was present, waiting for me to choose life or death. I thank God for Jesus Christ, the one who came to redeem mankind from the curse of the law.

John 6:37 says, "All that the Father giveth me shall come to me; and him that cometh to me I will in no wise cast out." What a wonderful invitation. My heart's door was wide open and Jesus entered and took up residence.

I gradually began to desire the things of God. Yes, I was timid but I said, "God, Jesus' disciples were too." The Holy Ghost came upon them one day and they were fearless and powerful. They went about praying and preaching the Word with boldness, resisting all opposition. Their enemies questioned, "Aren't these mere fishermen?" They never attended school yet what a transformation.

It was not easy but I kept on saying, if the disciples did it I can do all things through Christ which strengthens me. I use Philippians 4:13 as my motto or guiding principle and God stood by His Word to perform it. I began to hunger and thirst for the things of God, prayer and fasting were introduced to me by a friend and I was blessed. I struggled with this discipline but pressed through like the woman with the issue of blood.

> I can do all things through Christ which strengtheneth me.
> Philippians 4:13

> Blessed are they which do hunger and thirst after righteousness: for they shall be filled.
> Matthew 5:6

It's not easy to deny yourself food and water and then enter the throne of grace boldly. Oh, the great distraction and desire for the things of the flesh! It's a real battle but God rewards those who diligently seek Him. Prayer and fasting are two weapons that when coupled together will release the explosive power in your life to pull down the strongholds of Satan and his demons.

Jesus told His disciples that some of these things come not but by prayer and fasting. This information can be found in Mark 9:17-29, when the disciples failed to cast out a dumb and deaf that possessed a certain man's son.

The man brought his son to Jesus and He rebuked the spirits and charged them to come out the boy. They were commanded not to enter the boy again. The disciples needed an explanation why were they not able to cast out these spirits. Jesus told them that this kind can come forth by nothing, but prayer and fasting.

The Benefits of Fasting

The purpose of fasting is to attract the attention of God and not the attention of others. As a spiritual discipline, fasting can help us focus more intently on God, increasing our ability to concentrate mentally and increasing our sensitivity to the things of the spirit. Fasting helps us to concentrate on prayer. It heightens our spiritual awareness, lends intensity to our communion with God and reminds us of our weakness and our need for complete dependence on God.

I thank God that I'm an overcomer through Jesus Christ, who came to set me free from the wiles and fiery darts of the enemy. The Word of the Lord declares that no weapon formed against us shall prosper.

> No weapon that is formed against thee shall prosper; and every tongue that shall rise against thee in judgment, thou shalt condemn. This is the heritage of the servants of the Lord, and their righteousness is of me, saith the Lord.
> Isaiah 54:17

> Ye are of God, little children, and have overcome them; because greater is he that is in you than he that is in the world.
> 1 John 4:4

I desired the Word of God to overcome this dreaded phenomenon of the demonic and began to learn to pray the Word of God appropriately. I stood back and beheld God's intervention many times when I was attacked by the forces of darkness.

I decided not to desire the food that spoils but I sought the food that gives the eternal life that Jesus, the Son of the living God, gives us. I do thank God for His Word. Jesus used it to overcome the devil, and Satan was defeated every time. His Word is unchanging, therefore we can use it to defeat Satan, the accuser of the brethren.

> My son, attend to my words; incline thine ear unto my sayings. Let them not depart from thine eyes; keep them in the midst of thine heart. For they are life unto those that find them, and health to all their flesh.
> Proverbs 4:20-22

The Word of God tells us we need to seek wisdom. Only when we draw on His wisdom can we be certain that we will not perish for a lack of knowledge of the things we may encounter on our pilgrim pathway.

> Wisdom is the principal thing, therefore get wisdom. And with all of your getting, get understanding.
> Proverbs 4:7

> If any of you lack wisdom, let him ask of God, that giveth to all men liberally, and upbraideth not; and it shall be given him.
> James 1:5

For many years I struggled with the weird experiences I had with the demonic forces of darkness. I was not convinced demons were real until I became a Christian and began to study the Word of God. Many passages in the gospels refer to demons, and Jesus and His disciples had many encounters with evil spirits.

There are many people who do not believe in the existence of evil spirits or demons and therefore the devil and his demons have caused these people to harden their minds to the reality of the existence of demons. The Word of God declares that people perish because of a lack of knowledge.

> My people are destroyed for lack of knowledge: because thou hast rejected knowledge, I will also reject thee, that thou shalt be no priest to me: seeing that thou hast forgotten the law of my God, I will also forget my children.
> Hosea 4:6

Satan's best defense has been his success in deluding mankind into thinking he does not exist. If God's people allow Satan to deceive them, it simply proves how clever he is and how unbelievably naive humans can be. It's of paramount importance to know that there are three sources of power common to human understanding.

1) Divine power, or power that proceeds from the omnipotence of God. The Word of God declares in Colossians 2:10 that Jesus Christ is head of all principalities and powers and God's children who are called by His name are complete in Him.
2) Satanic power, or power that comes from Lucifer, the fallen archangel.
3) Human power, or the power of man, a neutral force that can be directed by heavenly or demonic power.

People sometimes ask where the devil and his demons come from. In John 1:3 the Word of God says, "All things were made by Him; and without Him was not anything made that was made." God is the creator of all, even the angelic beings. Therefore, God created Lucifer, highest of the order of the seraphim. God did not create a devil. Lucifer chose to make himself a devil.

Let's delve into the Word of God and see how such a drastic transformation took place.

> And there was a war in heaven and Michael and his angels fought against the dragon; and the dragon and his angels, and prevailed not; neither was there place found any more in heaven.
> Revelation 12:7-8

God is all powerful. No power or principality can defeat or supersede the power that proceeds from the omnipotence of the almighty God.

> Thy right hand, O Lord, is become glorious in power; Thy right hand, O Lord, hath dashed in pieces the enemy.
> Exodus 15:6

Who can withstand God? Absolutely nothing or no one! This great dragon—the old serpent, the devil—and his angels were cast out of heaven into the earth. Why were they excommunicated from heaven?

Lucifer was evidently the first created being, an archangel, and a member of the highest order of God's creation. He had the talent to create lovely music.

He was the anointed cherub—that is, he guarded God's throne. But instead of covering it, he coveted it and fell. Not content to be the beautiful, intelligent creature of God's creation and the highest order of angels, Satan aspired to a position of equality with God. He also wanted to be above God.

> Son of man, take up lamentation upon the king of Tyrus, and say unto him, thus sayeth the Lord God; thou sealest the sum, full of wisdom and perfect in beauty. Thou hast been in Eden the garden of God; every precious stone was thy covering, the sardius, topaz, and the diamond, the beryl, the onyx and the jasper, the sapphire, the emerald, and the carbuncle, and gold: the workmanship of thy tabrets and of thy pipes was prepared in the day that thou was created.
>
> Thou art the anointed cherub that covereth; and I have set thee so: thou wast up on the holy mountain of God; thou hast walked up and down in the midst of the stone of fire. Thou wast perfect in thy ways from the day that thou wast created, till iniquity was found in thee. By the multitude of thy merchandise they have filled the midst of thee with violence, and thou hast sinned: therefore I will cast thee as profane out of the mountain of God: and I will destroy thee, O covering cherub, from the midst of the stones of fire.
>
> Thine heart was lifted up because of thy beauty, thou hast corrupted thy wisdom by reason of thy brightness: I will cast thee to the ground, I will lay thee before kings, that they may behold thee. Thou hast defiled thy sanctuaries by the multitude of thy iniquities, by the iniquity of thy traffic; therefore will I bring forth a fire from the midst of thee, it shall devour thee and I will bring thee to ashes upon the earth in the sight of all them that behold thee. All they that know thee among the people shall be astonished at thee: thou shalt be a terror, and never shalt thou be any more.
>
> Ezekiel 28:12-19

In Isaiah 14:12-14, Satan uses the personal pronoun "I" five times. This reading tells us that Satan said to himself that he would establish a very high position for himself.

> How art thou fallen from heaven, O Lucifer, son of the morning! How art thou cut down to the ground, which didst weaken the nation! For thou hast said in thy heart, I will ascend into heaven, I will exalt my throne above the stars of God: I will sit also upon the mount of the congregation, in the sides of the north: I will ascend above the heights of the cloud; I will be like the most high.
>
> Isaiah 14:12-14

The devil would not be satisfied with anything other than the highest position in God's original creation. Pride caused his overthrow.

The Word of God declares in Proverbs 16:18 that pride goes before destruction and a haughty spirit before a fall. The middle letter of the word pride is "I", just as it is in sin, and it was the big "I" that brought about the fall of the divinely created and anointed cherub. Satan sinned against divine sovereignty and was thus cast out of heaven.

Revelation 12:4 relates an account of the dragon's tail (the devil) drawing one third of the stars of heaven to himself and casting them to the earth. Many commentators interpret stars as angels. Satan caused a third of the heavenly hosts to rebel along with him when he arrogantly tried to be like God. Satan is the recognized head of those angels. They are the demons, or the evil, unclean spirits, that the Bible speaks of. The word "demon" itself, however, is not found in the Bible. What is found in the Bible are many references to evil spirits or devils, which pervade the Scriptures from Genesis to Revelation. Let's take a look now at the various evil spirits spoken of throughout Scripture—spirits that are very much rampant in our day as well.

CHAPTER 5

Dealing with the Demonic

The word "demon" comes from the Latin word *daemon* (meaning evil spirit) and from the Greek word *daimon* (a divinity). The words evil spirit or unclean spirit is used 22 times in the New Testament. Let's take a look at a few examples.

> And there was in their synagogue a man with an unclean spirit and he cried out, saying, let us alone; what have we to do with thee, thou Jesus of Nazareth? Art thou come to destroy us? I know thee who thou art, the holy one of God. And Jesus rebuked him, saying, "Hold thy peace, and come out of him. And when the unclean spirit had torn him, and cried with a loud voice, he came out of him.
> Mark 1:23-25

> And as he was yet coming, the devil threw him down, and tare him. And Jesus rebuked the unclean spirit, and healed the child, and delivered him again to his father.
> Luke 9:42

> When the unclean spirit is gone out of a man, he walketh through dry places, seeking rest, and findeth none. Then he saith, I will return into my house from whence I came out; and when he is come, he findeth it empty, swept and garnished. Then goeth he, and taketh with himself seven other spirits more wicked than himself, and they enter in

a dwell there: And the last state of that man is worse than the first. Even so shall it be unto this wicked generation. Matthew 12:43-45

Other designations of demons or devils are:

1) Spirit of infirmity –And, behold, there was a woman which had a spirit of infirmity eighteen years, and was bowed together, and could in no wise lift up herself. And when Jesus saw her, he called her to him and said unto her, Woman thou art loosed from thine infirmity. And he laid his hand on her and immediately she was made straight, and glorified God. (Luke 13:11-13)
2) Dumb and Deaf Spirit – When Jesus saw that the people came running together, he rebuked the foul spirit, saying unto him, thou dumb and deaf spirit, I charge thee, come out of him, and enter no more into him. And the spirit cried and rent him sore, and came out of him: And he was as one dead; insomuch that many said he is dead. But Jesus took him by the hand, and lifted him up, and he arose. (Mark 9:25)
3) Blind Spirit – Then was brought unto him one possessed with a devil, blind, and dumb; And he healed him, insomuch that the blind and dumb both spake and saw. (Matthew 12:22)
4) Familiar Spirits – These are evil spirits who are familiar with a dead person's appearance, habits and life. They can imitate the deceased and therefore cause great deceit. Leviticus 20:27 states, "A man also or woman that hath a familiar spirit, or that is a wizard, shall surely be put to death: they shall stone them with stones: their blood shall be upon them."

And when they shall say unto you, seek unto them that have familiar spirits and unto wizards that peep, and that mutter: Should not a people seek unto their God? For the living to the dead?

Isaiah 8:19

Moreover the workers with familiar spirits, and the wizards, and the images, and the idols, and all the abominations that were spied in the land of Judah and in Jerusalem, did Josiah put away, that he might perform the words of the law which were written in the book that Hilkiah the priest found in the house of The Lord.

2 Kings 23:24

5) An Angel –And no marvel; for Satan himself is transformed into an angel of light. (2 Corinthians 11:14)

6) A Lying Spirit –And he said, I will go out, and be a lying spirit in the mouth of all his prophets. And the Lord said, thou shalt entice him, and thou shalt also prevail. Go out and do even so. Now therefore, behold, the Lord hath put a lying spirit in the mouth of these thy prophets and the Lord hath spoken evil against thee. (2 Chronicles 18:21-22)

7) Seducing Spirit – Now the spirit speaketh expressly, that in the latter times some shall depart from the faith, giving heed to seducing spirits, and doctrines of devils. (1 Timothy 4:1)

8) Foul Spirit – When Jesus saw that the people came running together, he rebuked the foul spirit, saying unto him, Thou dumb and deaf spirit, I charge thee, come out of him, and enter no more into him. (Mark 9:25)

And he cried mightily with a strong voice, saying, Babylon the great is fallen, is fallen, is become the habitation of devils, and the hold of every foul spirit, and a cage of every unclean and hateful bird.

Revelation 18:2

9) Jealous Spirit – Last but certainly not least, we will look at the spirit of jealousy.

And the spirit of Jealousy come upon him, and he be jealous of his wife, and she be defiled: Or when the spirit of Jealousy cometh upon him, and he be Jealous of his wife, and shall

set the woman before the Lord, and the priest shall execute upon her all this law.
Numbers 5:14, 30

It's evident from the Word of God that demons are real; they are not a fairytale or a myth. Demons are also ageless. From the Bible we understand that great numbers of demons roam the earth and the air. This is the response to the Lord's question in the book of Job, "From whence cometh thou?" Satan's response was "From going to and fro in the earth and from walking up and down in it."

Satan and his demons are not omnipresent but they are highly organized. This is apparent in the concluding passage of Paul's letter to the Ephesians.

For we wrestle not against flesh and blood, but against principalities, against powers, against rulers of the darkness of this world, against spiritual wickedness in high places.
Ephesians 6:12

Our archrival is the chief of fallen spirits or demons of the underworld, and he apparently controls other spirits who have rebelled against, and stand in opposition to, God. Satan rules over powerful kingdoms. The Word of God tells us that he was even bold enough to try to tempt Jesus.

That again the devil taketh him (Jesus) up into an exceeding high mountain and sheweth him all the kingdoms of the world, and the glory of them; And (the devil) sayeth unto him (Jesus), all these will I give thee, if thou wilt fall down and worship me.
Matthew 4:8-9

Jesus didn't succumb to what the devil offered, He knew the kingdoms, the power and the glory belong to Jehovah God forever.

Satan and his demons have their abode and base of operation in the high places. It's of great interest therefore for God's people to understand that demons do not die; they have been in the world since the beginning of time. Demons are personalities without bodies—inhuman, yet seeking human possession in order to manifest themselves. They can use the person's voice or throat to speak. Under the influence of demonic power a man can speak with the voice of a woman, a woman can also speak with the gruff voice of a man. Demons are angry with God because of their fallen state, their prime motive is to destroy what God loves or creates – chiefly, man.

The Word of God declares that even though the devil might come to devastate us, Jesus is our lifegiver. 1John 3:8 tells us that for this purpose was the son of God manifested, that He might destroy the works of the devil. Likewise, John 10:10 says, "The thief (devil) cometh not, but to steal, and to kill and to destroy I am come that they might have life, and that they might have it more abundantly."

As children of God we cannot give the devil and his demons a foothold in our lives. We have to clothe ourselves at all times with the spiritual armor of God. The helmet of salvation has to be worn on the head so that our thinking processes aren't warped by his suggestions and lies. The breastplate of righteousness for the heart (where the affections are centered) protects us from the inroads of lesser love. We are to love God more than anything or anyone else. Then other loves come into proper perspective.

Our loins must be girded about with truth. This means Jesus can control, with our willingness, even the unruly areas of our lives. Our feet need to be shod with the preparation of the gospel of peace; our feet symbolize our comings and our goings as well as the call to stand firm in the faith.

The sword of the Spirit, which is the unadulterated, active Word of God, must be implanted in the hearts of God's children. Only then will the Holy Spirit be able to bring that Word to us and impress it upon our spirit. The Word is the only offensive weapon we can use, as Jesus did, to put to flight the temptations of the devil.

God's people need to be well versed in the scriptures so they can say to the devil "it is written" and send him off with his lies. One cannot forget the shield of faith and prayer. The shield of faith enables us as children of God to trust that the accusations of the devil need not find us vulnerable. Faith in Christ's righteousness, not our own, enables us to fearlessly face the enemy of our soul and deflect his arrows.

Then we ought to pray always in the spirit. Prayer is like a match that is used to release the explosive power of the Holy Spirit in the affairs of His people. Spirit-authored prayer springs from the mind of Christ (indeed, we have the mind of Christ) and reaches the heart of God. His answers enable us to walk where His Spirit leads and with sharp discernment know what is of God, what is of the devil and what is of the flesh.

If we aren't dressed according to the Word of God, demons will invade our lives. They are intelligent and wise angelic beings. They roam to and fro seeking a vulnerable soul to destroy or lie to. Demons cannot walk in to take possession of just any person's life, they must find someone with an open door. If he is a spirit of lust, he seeks a lustful person, a person with a strong or depraved desire or great longing for things that are wrong. If the demon is a spirit of anger, he seeks to possess a person who has little control over his temper. A spirit of insanity will seek to destroy a person's mind.

Demons are powerful but not almighty. Mark 5:1-18 tells us that when Jesus and His disciples left the ship in the land of the Gardarenes they encountered the demoniac of Gadara, a man with a legion of devils within him. The Word of God tells us this man made his dwelling among the tombs and no man was strong enough to bind him with chains. This demon-possessed man was so strong that his chains were plucked asunder and broken in pieces many times by him. He was ferocious and night and day he was in the mountains and in the tombs crying and cutting himself with stones. According to the Bible, everyone was afraid of this man. They even feared to pass by him. Strangers and visitors took another road because of this wild man.

When Jesus came by, the Creator of all things, the One who was manifested to destroy the works of the devil, this demoniac roared out against him. He wanted to destroy Jesus but Jesus confronted him and let him know things were going to be the other way around. Jesus asked him, "What is your name?" The spirit identified himself as Legion: "for we are many." Jesus commanded them to come out. There is no power in the heavens and under the earth that can supersede the power that is upon Jesus. Greater is He that is in us than he that is in the world. Jesus said God had sent Him to minister to the downtrodden.

> The spirit of the Lord is upon me, because he hath anointed me to preach the gospel to the poor; He hath sent me to heal the broken-hearted, to preach deliverance to the captives, and recovering of sight to the blind, to set at liberty them that are bruised.
>
> Luke 4:18

Everywhere Jesus went demons were cast out, silenced and many were delivered. The Word of the Lord says in James 4:7; "so then, submit to God. Resist the devil and he will run away from us." Jesus is our commander and loving champion; every knee shall bow and every tongue shall confess that Jesus Christ is Lord.

Demons have knowledge but they are not omniscient.

> And behold they cried out saying: What have we to do with thee, Jesus, Thou son of God? Art thou come hither to torment us before the time?
>
> Matthew 8:29

> And devils came out of many, crying out and saying: Thou art the Christ the son of God. And he rebuking them suffered them not to speak. For they knew that he was the Christ.
>
> Luke 4:41

> Then certain of the vagabond Jews, exorcists, took upon them to call over them which had evil spirits the name of the Lord Jesus, saying, we adjure you by Jesus whom Paul preacheth. And there were seven sons of one Scé-va, a Jew, and chief of the priests, which did so. And the evil spirit answered and said: Jesus I know, and Paul I know; but who are ye? And the man in whom the evil spirit was leaped on them, and overcame them, and prevailed against them, so that they fled out of that house naked and wounded.
>
> Acts 19:13-16

Evil spirits have not lost their knowledge or intelligence; they are the same today as they were in the New Testament era. They knew who my mom was and they cried out several times in prayer meetings saying, "I'm not afraid of that man, but I'm afraid of that lady."

My neighbor had a demonic invasion many years ago so they summoned my mother. She was cooking that particular evening and I was very hungry, having just arrived home from school. She wasn't hesitant at all. She hurriedly went with the neighbors.

They told her stones were being thrown on the house and the inside of the house had caught fire. My mother wasn't afraid of the forewarning or the uproar. She stepped over onto Satan's turf and immediately the stones and fire disappeared. Demons know who we are, and we ought to know Jesus so that when we are confronted or besieged by them the Holy Spirit will take up a standard for us.

Isaiah 59:19; so shall they fear the name of the Lord from the west, and his glory from the rising of the sun. When the enemy shall come in like a flood, the Spirit of the Lord shall lift up a standard against him.

Evil spirits or demons possess people and cause diseases, dumbness, deafness and blindness.

The New Testament contains several accounts of how Jesus cast out evil spirits.

> When Jesus saw that the people came running together, he rebuked the foul spirit, saying unto him, thou dumb and deaf spirit, I charge thee, come out of him, and enter no more into him.
>
> Mark 9:25

> As they went out, behold, they brought to him (Jesus) a dumb man possessed with a devil. And when the devil was cast out, the dumb spake: and the multitude marveled, saying, it was never so seen in Israel.
>
> Matthew 9:32-33

Then was brought unto him (Jesus) one possessed with a devil, blind, and dumb: and he healed him, insomuch that the blind and dumb both spake and saw.
Matthew 12:22

Demons are the cause of many diseases, but not all diseases can be attributed to demons.

And Jesus went about all Galilee, teaching in their synagogues and preaching the gospel of the kingdom, and healing all manner of sickness and all manner of disease among the people. And his fame went throughout all Syria: and they brought unto him all sick people that were taken with diverse diseases and torments, and those which were possessed with devils and those which were lunatic and those that had the palsy; and he healed them.
Matthew 4:23-24

Evil spirits also cause grievous vexation, suicide, lunacy and mania.

Grievous Vexation

And when they were come to the multitude, there came to him a certain man, kneeling down to him, and saying, Lord, have mercy on my son: for he is lunatic and sore vexed: for often times he falleth into the fire, and oft into the water. And I brought him to Thy disciples, and they could not cure him.

Then Jesus answered and said, O faithless and perverse generation, how long shall I be with you? How long shall I suffer you? Bring him hither to me.

And Jesus rebuked the devil; and he departed from him: And the child was cured from that hour. Then came the disciples to Jesus apart, and said, why could not we cast him out? And Jesus said unto them, because of your unbelief: For verily I say unto you, if ye have faith as a grain of mustard seed, ye shall say unto the mountain, remove hence to yonder place; and it shall remove; and nothing shall be impossible unto you. Howbeit this kind goeth not out but by prayer and fasting.

Matthew 17:14-21

Suicide

And they came over unto the other side of the sea, into the country of the Gadarenes and when he was come out of the ship, immediately there met him out of the tombs a man with an unclean spirit, who had his dwelling among the tombs; and no man could bind him, no, not with chains: because that he had been often bound with fetters and chains, and the chains had been plucked asunder by him, and the fetters broken in pieces: neither could any man tame him. And always, night and day, he was in the mountains, and in the tombs, crying and cutting himself with stones. But when he saw Jesus afar off, he ran and worshipped him, and cried with a loud voice, and said, what have I to do with thee, Jesus, thou Son of the most high God? I adjure you by God, that thou torment me not. For he said unto him, come out of the man, thou unclean spirit.

Mark 5:1-8

And they brought him unto him: And when he saw him, straightway the spirit tare him; And he fell to the ground, and wallowed foaming.

Mark 9:20

Evil spirits or demons can oppress, be jealous, steal, fight, tell fortunes, possess man at will, travel and imitate the departed dead.

But the spirit of the Lord departed from Saul, and an evil spirit from the Lord troubled him.

1 Samuel 16:14

How God anointed Jesus of Nazareth with the Holy Ghost and with power: Who went about doing good, and healing all that were oppressed of the devil: for God was with him.
Acts 10:38

Those by the wayside are they that hear; then cometh the devil, and taketh away the word out of their hearts, lest they should believe and be saved.
Luke 8:12

A man also, or woman that hath a familiar spirit, or that is a wizard, shall surely be put to death: they shall stone them with stones: their blood shall be upon them.
Leviticus 20:27

So Saul died for his transgression which he committed against the Lord, even against the word of the Lord, which he kept not, and also for asking counsel of one who had a familiar spirit, to enquire of it.
1 Chronicles 10:13

Evil spirits or demons can cause error, deceptions, lying, witchcraft, heresies, fable-teaching and prophecies.

Now the spirit speaketh expressly, that in the latter times some shall depart from the faith, giving heed to seducing spirits, and doctrines of devils; speaking lies in hypocrisy; having their conscience scared with a hot iron.
1 Timothy 4:1-2

Beloved, believe not every spirit, but try the spirits whether they are of God: Because many false prophets are gone out into the world. Hereby know ye the spirit of God: Every spirit that confesseth that Jesus Christ is come in the flesh is of God. And every spirit that confesseth not that Jesus Christ is come in the flesh is not of God: And this is the spirit of Antichrist, whereof ye have heard that it should come; and even now already is it in the world. Ye are of God, little children, and have overcome them: Because greater is he that is in you, than ye that is in the world. They are of the world: Therefore, speak they of the world, and the world heareth them. We are of God: He that knoweth God heareth us; He that is not of God heareth not us. Hereby know we that spirit of truth, and the spirit of error.

1 John 4:1-6

And he caused his children to pass through the fire in The Valley of the Son of Hin-nom: Also he observed times, and used enchantments, and used witchcraft, and dealt with a familiar spirit, and with wizards: He wrought much evil in the sight of the Lord, to provoke him to anger.

2 Chronicles 33:6

And there came forth a spirit, and stood before the Lord, and said, I will persuade him. And the Lord said unto him, wherewith? And he said, I will go forth, and I will be a lying spirit in the mouth of all his prophets. And he said, thou shalt persuade him, and prevail also: Go forth, and do so. Now therefore, behold, the Lord hath put a lying spirit in the mouth of all these thy prophets, and the Lord hath spoken evil concerning thee.

1 Kings 22:21-23

When the unclean spirit is gone out of a man, he walketh through dry places, seeking rest, and findeth none. Then he saith, I will return into my house from whence I came out; and when he is come, he findeth it empty, swept and garnished. Then goeth he, and taketh with himself seven other spirits more wicked than himself, and they enter in and dwell there: And the last state of that man is worse than the first. Even so shall it be unto this wicked generation.

Matthew 12:43-45

Demons wage war on saints, influence men, have unbelievers in league with them and inflict physical maladies on those they possess.

And you hath he quickened, who were dead in trespasses and sins; wherein in time past he walked according to the course of this world, according to the prince of the power of the air, the spirit that now worketh in the children of disobedience: among whom also we all had our conversation in times past in the lust of our flesh, fulfilling the desires of the flesh and of the mind: and were by nature the children of wrath, even as others.
Ephesians 2:1-3

Finally, my brethren, be strong in the Lord, and in the power of his might. Put on the whole armor of God, that we may ye able to stand against the wiles of the devil. For we wrestle not against flesh and blood, but against principalities, against powers, against the rulers of darkness of this world, against spiritual wickedness in high places. Wherefore take unto you the whole armor of God that ye may be able to withstand in the evil day, and having done all, to stand. Stand therefore, having your loins, girt about with truth, and having on the breastplate of righteousness; and your feet shod with the preparation of peace: above all, taking the shield of faith, wherewith ye shall be able to quench all the fiery darts of the wicked. And take the element of salvation, and the sword of the spirit, which is the word of God: praying always with all prayer and supplication in the spirit, and watching thereunto with all perseverance and supplication for all saints.
Ephesians 6:10-18

CHAPTER 6

Dealing with Witchcraft

The study of evil spirits, demons, the devil and so forth eventually leads to the subject of witchcraft. The word "witch" is derived from the Indo-European root word *weik,* which means religion and magic. The word "witchcraft" comes from the old English term *wicce-craft,* which refers to the art or skill of using supernatural forces to bend one's will. Witchcraft is mentioned several times in the Bible. In 1 Samuel 15:23 the Word of the Lord says that rebellion is as the sin of witchcraft and stubbornness is as iniquity and idolatry. Therefore, witchcraft is rebellion coupled with a desire to "stay in the game," to be a spiritual player without submitting to God. Witchcraft starts with a heart of rebellion and works by focusing on a distraction, a lie that is some technique purported to release demonic power by focusing the victim on something other than the subject at hand.

What is magic? Magic is the art of using hidden power. Witchcraft is a religion that worships Satan and his demonic forces in order to receive magic power to influence the wills of others. It is sometimes referred to as the religion of Wicca. Death is glorified at various levels in the cult of witchcraft. In the beginning stages a person might sacrifice frogs, cats, or birds, but the highest order of sacrifice is that of a human being. Through killing, witches seek to please Satan and release his evil power.

Back in Jamaica I often wondered about people who killed chickens and sprinkled the blood around their homes and businesses.

I didn't understand what they were doing and what it meant to them. I now understand it was done for protection.

From ancient times those who try to manipulate the spirit world have used human sacrifice—the most dreaded and most powerful of all sacrifices. If a god gave assistance to humanity in exchange for the sacrifice of a goat or a bull, it was reasoned, a human sacrifice or life would buy stronger favor.

In 2 Chronicles 28 King Ahaz tried to buy the help of the nature god of Canaan with the life of his son in a time of national and personal crisis.

> There shall not be found among you any one that maketh his son or his daughter to pass through the fire, or that useth divination, or an observer of times, or an enchanter or a witch, or a charmer, or a consulter with familiar spirit, or a wizard or a necromancer. For all that do these things are an abomination unto the Lord: And because of these abominations the Lord thy God doth drive them out from before thee.
>
> Deuteronomy 18:10-12

The Many Positions and Practices of the Art of Witchcraft

It is of paramount importance to know these positions and their roles in Satan's kingdom. Let's look at the definitions.

> *Divination:* the practice of using the stars and evil spirits to foretell the future.
>
> *Observers of Times:* a term used many times in the Bible, referring to astrology. In astrology, one observes the movement of the sun, moon, stars and planets to predict the future of man.
>
> *Enchanter:* one who casts spells upon people to control their actions. What is the meaning of spells? The term refers to the act of calling up a demon and then sending it to the person to perform certain influences or damage. All spells

are accomplished by demons, even the so-called "good" ones such as those stimulating love in a person.

Witch: a woman enchanter who has great demonic powers.

Charmer: a hypnotist who charms the mind and will of another person to gain control.

Consulter with Familiar Spirits: a witch or enchanter who uses an animal to carry out an evil deed against another person.

Wizard: one who uses magic or sorcery to control the will of others. What is sorcery? It's magic or witchcraft.

Necromancer: one who supposedly communicates with the dead.

All of these practices are condemned by God and have at their root evil deeds or death. These practices, both in the days of old and even now, displease God. Men tend to forget the God of wisdom and seek out hidden things from the gods of this universe. They have rejected the wisdom, knowledge and understanding of God and resort to the lies of the devil. He is a trickster and the father of all lies.

God's purpose is to destroy and cut off those who practice such dark arts.

And the soul that turneth after such as have familiar spirits, and after wizards, to go a whoring after them, I will even set my face against that soul, and will cut him off from among his people.
Leviticus 20:6

Thou shalt not suffer a witch to live.
Exodus 22:18

And when they shall say unto you, seek unto them that have familiar spirits and unto wizards that peep, and that mutter:

should not a people seek unto their God? For the living to the dead?

Isaiah 8:19

Even the righteous can be persuaded to use demonic powers. We should never underestimate demonic powers, for even great servants of God such as King Saul were persuaded to use evil to gain information. Saul was chosen by God to be the first king of Israel because the Israelites rejected God as their leader.

Saul's first great failure occurred when he disobeyed the Word of God spoken by Samuel.

And thou shalt go down before me to Gilgal; and, behold, I will come down unto thee, to offer burnt offerings, and to sacrifice sacrifices of peace offering: seven days shalt thou tarry, till I come to thee, and show thee what thou shalt do.

1 Samuel 10:8

Saul's excuse was that sacrifice had to be offered to guarantee success in the battle. Meanwhile, as Samuel delayed his appearance, Saul's army was deserting him. He waited until the seventh day, but couldn't bring himself to wait till that day was over. Saul, a Benjamite, offered the burnt offering that only a Levite and priest might offer (Numbers 16:1-40). This act was a direct violation of God's law, an act of rebellion against God by God's representative. It was proof of the disbelief of his heart and his essential unfitness to be king over God's people.

Saul's second great folly was sparing the life of Agag the king of the Amalekites and saving his choicest sheep and cattle and the fattest lambs, everything of high value, when God had told the Israelites to destroy the Amalekites and all their goods. In the face of this open disobedience to the Word of God, the Lord told Samuel that he was sorry he had allowed Saul to be king.

Saul's life was headed in the right direction but he eventually chose the wrong way. God is said to repent when a change in the character and conduct of those with whom He is dealing leads to a corresponding change in His purposes and plans for them.

Samuel consulted Saul and reminded him that it was God who anointed him king over Israel. He asked, "Why then, did you not listen to the Lord's voice, but flung yourself on the loot and did evil in the Lord's sight?"

> And Samuel said, hath the Lord as great delight in burnt offerings and sacrifices, as in obeying the voice of the Lord? Behold, to obey is better than sacrifice, and to hearken than the fat of rams.
> 1 Samuel 15:22

> For I desired mercy, and not sacrifice; and the knowledge of God more than burnt offerings.
> Hosea 6:6

Faith in God's Word that produces obedience to God's will delight the Lord. Burnt offerings and sacrifices may indicate mere external adherence to religion or even hypocrisy, but obedience to God springs out of the heart, for rebellion is as the sin of witchcraft. The sin of divination consists of sin against the Word of God by consulting with some other being in opposition to God or by neglecting His Word.

Eventually Samuel died and was not available for consultation by Saul. Saul inquired of the Lord about the outcome of a battle he was about to have with the Philistines but received no answer, either by dreams or by the urim, the sacred lots, or by the prophets. So, Saul, the king who put those who were mediums and wizards out of the land, resorted to the spiritualistic medium of Endor (see 1 Samuel 28).

Accordingly, he who himself was demonized consulted with demonic powers to ascertain what to do about the battle. Saul commanded his servants to seek a woman who was a medium—a woman with familiar spirit or a divining demon. He then asked that Samuel be brought up from the realm of the spirits, because he knew there was no one who knew future events as well as this venerable prophet and judge.

The woman doubtlessly began her customary preparations for her control, by entering into a trancelike state in order to summon the demon who then proceeded to impersonate the individual called for.

Something strange and frightening happened to the witch of Endor. The usual occult procedure was abruptly cut short with the sudden and unexpected appearance of the spirit of Samuel. She screamed out with shock as she perceived that God had stepped in.

By God's power and permission, Samuel's spirit was presented to pronounce final doom upon Saul. Samuel's rebuke to Saul is added evidence that his spirit had actually appeared and it was not an impersonating demon.

In the severest terms Samuel announced that the Lord had wrestled the kingdom from Saul and that Saul and his sons would die the next day. Saul's last act of lawlessness—resorting to necromancy—resulted in his untimely end on the battlefield. May we as God's people always seek the guidance of the living God rather than that of the witch of Endor.

> Trust in the Lord with all thine heart; and lean not to thine own understanding. In all thy ways acknowledge him, and he shall direct thy paths.
>
> Proverbs 3:5-6

That particular encounter with the demonic forces of darkness is mentioned only in the Old Testament but everywhere Jesus went demons were rampant. The most interesting thing about Jesus was that He healed all who were oppressed of the devil, for God was with Him.

> How God anointed Jesus of Nazareth with the Holy Ghost and with power: who went about doing good, and healing all that were oppressed of the devil; for God was with him.
>
> Acts 10:38

It's very important to search the scriptures, because we will often find an account or accounts of those who dabbled in the art of witchcraft and what their experiences were.

As a result of the great persecution of the church in Jerusalem the apostles were scattered abroad and everywhere they went the Word was preached. Unclean spirits couldn't tolerate the penetrating sharpness of the Word, they cried with loud voice and came out of many people who were possessed. What a great joy that was! God's power was evidently at work and Satan's power was also very effective among the people.

In Acts 8:9-24; the Bible presents an account of a powerful wizard or spiritual leader by the name of Simon Magus. He used his deceptive power of sorcery over a community made up of 70,000 people. Were there no Christians living there? Let's find out! Acts 8:10-11 says that from the least unto the greatest of men, all gave heed unto Simon because of the length of time he had bewitched them.

Jesus was the Lamb of God sent to sacrifice His life so that through Him we will have the victory over all the powers of darkness. According to the scripture in 1 John 3:8; the Son of God was manifested to destroy the works of the devil. This same Jesus was preached by a chosen vessel of honor named Philip.

Philip was one of the seven deacons chosen in Acts 6 to settle Grecians dispute. Many believed this dynamic message proclaimed by this anointed vessel, including the great wizard. Signs and wonders followed Philip's message.

Simon was confused because he hadn't seen such a demonstration of Spirit and power. His eyes were fastened on the apostles. Nothing missed him including the laying on of the apostle's hands and the reception of the Holy Ghost by those touched. This, in fact, caused Simon to covet the power of God and prompted him to offer money for the power. Nothing is wrong with wanting to see the power of God manifested in our lives, but destruction is in store for anyone who thinks they can buy it.

What a deception and presumptuousness! Had Simon really believed the Word of God? No, he pretended to be a changed person so he could lay hold of this supernatural power. He was sharply rebuked by Peter and he begged the man of God to pray for him.

Satan's mediums and power cannot stand the supreme power of God the Father and His Son Jesus Christ. Jesus said all power is given unto Him in heaven and earth. God's children are partakers of this divine power.

His Word says, in Luke 10:19; "Behold, I have given you authority over scorpions and serpents and power over the enemy and no harm shall befall thee." God's people need to come to the realization that these arts are still prevalent today and are at work in our churches, schools and homes. Sorcery can work in many forms and can result in the total destruction of people's lives, emotional problems and mental breakdowns, financial problems, accidents, constant family feuds and suicidal youth.

Elymas the Sorcerer

Acts chapter 13 says, that as the people of Jesus gathered to minister to the Lord the Holy Ghost told them to separate Barnabas and Saul for the work they were called to do. Verse 6 states that when they had gone through the isle, unto Pa'-phos, they found a certain sorcerer, a false prophet, a Jew whose name was Bar-Jesus. Bar-Jesus in Aramaic means "son of salvation" but, he was, in fact, a magician and false prophet.

In essence he was a magician or astrologer attached to the political entourage as an adviser to the governor Sergius Paulus. It was Sergius Paulus who summoned Barnabas and Saul because he desired to hear the Word of God. In Acts 13:8 Elymas withstood Barnabas, Saul and Sergius Paulus seeking to turn away the deputy from the faith.

As he sensed that the governor was accepting the message of Barnabas and Saul, he realized his own position would be endangered. How could Elymas have swayed the governor from hearing God's Word? One simple incantation could have assigned a demon to the governor to begin a battle in his mind to resist the Word.

Sometimes the Word is received but in no time the devil steals it. He is a thief. The Word of the Lord declares in Mark 4:14-15 that the sower sows the Word. And these are they by the wayside, where the Word is sown; but when they have heard, Satan comes immediately, and takes away the Word sown in their hearts.

Barnabas and Saul, filled with the Holy Ghost, could discern that there was an opposing force emanating from Elymas. Paul rebuked

Elymas sharply and called him a child of the devil and enemy of all righteousness. He rebuked his perversion of truth and struck him with temporary blindness. Elymas sought someone to lead him by the hand. I believe it is very important to note that the gift of discerning of spirits was operable in the life of the apostle Paul, so he knew that a demonic spirit was interfering with the work of the Lord.

Let us look at this word discern. What does it mean? It means to distinguish clearly, to behold as separate. Discerning of spirits is the ability the Holy Spirit gives to some Christians to discern between those who speak by the Spirit of God and those who are moved by false spirits.

The phrase "discerning of spirits" occurs in 1 Corinthians 12:10 as one of the gifts of the Spirit. This is what the Word of the Lord says, to another the working of miracles; to another prophecy; to another discerning of spirits; to another divers kinds of tongues; to another the interpretation of tongues.

The discerning of spirits shows which gifts of the Holy Spirit are operating in a service. Some Christians are able to distinguish how God is working and how evil spirits are working. It is imperative that we allow the gift to operate so that the body of Christ can gain power and authority over demonic spirits. This gift is entrusted to the body of Christ for the perfecting of saints, for the work of the ministry, for the edifying of the body of Christ.

Amazed and stunned by the power of these servants of the Lord over his resident magician, Sergius Paulus believed the doctrine of the Lord. The enemy has power to sway us from the things of God but God's power is greater to pull down and render ineffective the powers of darkness.

2 Corinthians 10:4-5; for the weapons of our warfare are not carnal, but mighty through God to the pulling down of strongholds; Casting down imaginations, and every high thing that exalteth itself against the knowledge of God, and bringing into captivity every thought to the obedience of Christ.

Christians can be very judgmental of people who resist the gospel – the good news of Christ Jesus, so let us not be ignorant of the devils' ploy to buffet the mind.

But if our gospel is hid, it is hid to them that are lost: In whom the God of this world hath blinded the minds of them which believe not, lest the light of the glorious Gospel of Christ, who is the image of God, should shine unto them.
2 Corinthians 4:3-4

We are destroyed because of the lack of knowledge. Let us purpose in our hearts to be filled with the Holy Spirit so that the enemy will be resisted at all times. James 4:7 tells us to resist the devil and he will flee from you. He will have to flee when we call upon the name of Jesus Christ of Nazareth.

CHAPTER 7

God's Eccentrics

In the country of Haiti witch doctors are very popular. The religion of the nation is called voodoo. Voodoo witch doctors blew dust on their followers to put them into a spirit of Zambia, making them zombies. Zombies, although alive, are actually in a deep sleep and appear to be dead.

A group of people were invited to go and pray to break this Zambia spell. They were taken to morgues full of refrigerators in which lay bodies with tagged feet on tables. They were told that even though they appeared to be dead, every person in that room was alive. Most of those who came to pray didn't make it out. They began to call upon the name of the Lord when all of a sudden there was a kind of whirlwind effect and everyone was knocked to the ground. Someone cried out, "Jesus, cover us under your blood!" A renowned minister who was part of the group said, "I was not prepared for this kind of battle then, but now the eyes of my understanding are opened to the powers of darkness. I'm now equipped to withstand the devil."

> And I sought for a man among them that should make up the hedge, and stand in the gap before me for the land, that I should not destroy it, but I found none.
>
> Ezekiel 22:30

God's greatest desire is for men and women to call upon Him. Some of the vessels He chooses to use are quite eccentric. What is meant by eccentric? It's being odd or peculiar; one who defies the social conventions; departure from the normal way of conducting oneself.

The word eccentric is appropriate to describe John the Baptist, the forerunner of Jesus Christ whose parents were very old when he was born. Luke's account tells us that John was born filled with the Holy Ghost. From the time he was conceived he was anointed for a prophetic assignment.

John's ministry was sovereignly directed by God. It's written in the Bible that John was a joy and delight to his parents and many rejoiced because of his birth. He was great in the sight of God and he was never to take wine or fermented drink. This act showed his special dedication to God.

John's dress code was not in vogue. He wore camel's hair, with a leather belt around his waist. His diet was locusts and wild honey. Though peculiar, he was on a mission for the Lord. His mission was twofold: to prepare the way for the coming of the Messiah and to call the world to repentance. He conveyed his message in the spirit and power of Elijah.

Can you imagine John shaking like a reed endowed with power? He said, "After me will come one more powerful than I, the thongs of whose sandals I am not worthy to stoop down and untie." He also said "I baptize you with water, but He will baptize you with the Holy Ghost and fire." John's message brought many people to the Lord their God. His message had an impact on the people. It was life changing. The word he spoke turned the hearts of the father to their children and the disobedient to the wisdom of the righteous, thus preparing a people for the Lord.

John the Baptist was not impressed with those who were steeped in their sin. His rebuke was sharp, open and very blunt. As a result of his distaste for Herods' presumptuous sin he was beheaded, but his mission was realized. He said, with confidence, "I must decrease for Christ to increase" or establish His ministry. Had John been a 21st century prophet, he would have been considered a crazy or mentally ill person.

Is there anyone as eccentric as John the Baptist living in the 21st Century? I'm pretty sure there are people out there who are crazy for

Jesus but they have to be discovered. Persons or vessels of John's caliber will not be found in the crowds or gatherings we are used to. John lived in the wilderness but he preached to the people. We do not always understand the manifestation of the Holy Ghost. We cannot figure him out, but varied gifts are given to God's people to edify the body of Christ.

In my case, after I had prayed for myself and was prayed for many times, my condition remained the same. I never stopped offering up prayer to God like the sweet-smelling fragrance of incense but it was discouraging at times because it seemed as if God wasn't listening to me. Nevertheless, I lay hold of His Word which says He will never give me more than I can bear.

1 Corinthians 10:13; states, there hath no temptation taken you but such as is common to man: but God is faithful, who will not suffer you to be tempted above that ye are able; but will with the temptation also make a way of escape, that ye may be able to bear it. I was buffeted by the enemy but I stood my ground and waited patiently for him.

One day I bumped into a friend who said she would like me to meet a lady she had met some time ago. She warned me that I might have to try the spirit because this woman was quite different. I pondered the comment about her being different but I was interested in meeting her. I made many attempts to see her without success, so I decided to wait a little longer. I realized that nothing can be done before God's timing. After a period of time, I called my friend and she decided to take me see this woman. Anxious, I asked if she had told the woman I was coming. She told me no, but said we should just show up with my friends and it would better that way when they are convinced that God is able to do the impossible.

When I reached the church, the people were on fire like those people in the upper room, but I decided not to be distracted. I carefully observed everything that happened. I listened attentively to the Word of God and the songs they sang and then we began to worship. The people were warm-hearted and caring so I felt at home. After I was warmly welcomed the woman asked if she had ever met me. I said no. She said, "You're praying to God for your family but don't worry, God is going to turn everything around." She said, "One may chase a thousand but two put ten thousand to flight."

A pastor, this woman is indeed a peculiar person and her ways of doing things are most of the time quite odd. She has the fierceness of a lion when she is worshipping God. Everyone has to worship the Lord with all their hearts or be prepared to be sent home. She is crazy for Jesus and she has reason to be. She was diagnosed with cancer of the abdomen and should have died, but she believed in the prayer of faith. Many believers had confidence in God and laid their hands on her, prayed sincerely, then all of a sudden this woman vomited mucous and other particles from her belly and she was completely healed. What a healer Jesus is! A vessel of honor for Jesus, she is a real threat to the devil and his cohorts. People from many nations have experienced the healing power of Jesus through her. Many members of her church are people whom Satan has ravaged but who were delivered by the power of God.

We dare not say these encounters are mythical. If Satan bound people when Christ was on earth, he still has power to ensnare people now. For instance, a middle-aged woman named Mary Jane gave the following account of demonic invasion. She said the witches or wizards had bewitched her since she was very young and as a result of their curse she hadn't excelled in school. This is quite believable; I've known of many people who had similar experiences.

Mary Jane's worst encounter with the demonic occurred after her parents died in Jamaica and left their property to be shared among their children. Mary Jane went home to Jamaica and her brother was very unpleasant to her. How could her own flesh and blood consult a servant of Satan to inflict physical maladies on his own sister? The heart of a man is deceitfully wicked; who can understand it?

Mary Jane's brother didn't want to give her her share of the land; therefore he was determined to destroy her. When she returned home to Canada, she was crippled on the left side. She couldn't do anything for herself. She lost her job and went on welfare and disability. How much worse could it get? Her life wasn't worth living and she was on the verge of giving up when God stepped in. We know He's an on-time God; He may seem to set out late, but He always arrives on time.

Mary Jane was also invited to the church to see the same woman of God I had seen, the woman who was crazy for Jesus. This vessel of honor said to her, "Woman, lift your hands and praise God." She knew she couldn't lift her hands but she obeyed and was healed. She said, "I couldn't help but praise God. He delivered me from the power of darkness. We do have treasures in earthen vessels to show forth the power of God." 2Corinthians 4:7; but we have this treasure in earthen vessels that the Excellency of the power may be of God, and not of us.

The apostle Paul spoke about a demonstration of God's power and Spirit. Nothing less will be able to conquer the unconquerable, make possible the impossible, loose the bands of wickedness and set the prisoners of Satan free.

Where are the vessels that are possessed, saturated and endowed by the power of God to loose those that are bound? Lord, prepare us to be a sanctuary for your glory.

Another member of this woman's church told her story. She said that at a certain point in her life she felt as if she was never alone, but the presence she felt was quite evil. At times she felt something lying on her and she couldn't see what it was. I have had this experience also and it is quite frightening.

This young lady was asthmatic and had a problem in her abdominal cavity. Sometimes her tummy was as flat as a pancake and at other times she could be mistaken for a pregnant woman. In fact, many people did think she was pregnant. She was not alarmed, since she thought that was the way the body worked at times. It so happened that she met a lady who asked her if she was pregnant. She told the woman she was not. The woman told her, "You need to meet my pastor. She will help you."

Curious, she went to church that following Sunday morning and was ministered to. The young lady reports that the pastor and her prayer team prayed for her and she was set free, never to be bound again by the power of darkness. Whomever Jesus sets free is free indeed. He came to destroy the works of the devil, and as saints in Christ we are complete in Him who is the head of all principalities and powers.

Being peculiar or eccentric for Jesus is an awesome thing. I personally experienced the working of the spirit of Zambia in my life during my ordeal in Jamaica. All I wanted to do was to sleep all the time. I had difficulty staying up. I slept everywhere and anywhere, standing, lying down and kneeling. When I woke up I was always drained and weary. Could I have understood what I was going through then? Absolutely not! I had not known about such things of the spirit and their effect on human beings.

Don't be ignorant of the devil's wiles. The devil's wiles are attractive, deceptive and ensnaring. Satan is a personal enemy, a great adversary, a slanderous accuser and a malignant foe. He uses clever and crafty methods to deceive.

We also know that he can use mankind to accomplish his plan but what we have to bear in our minds is the Word of the Lord in Ephesians 6:12-18. He is the god of this world and he is very crafty. He is full of wisdom according to Ezekiel 28.

God's Word declares that the Spirit of the Lord will help us withstand the devil's power.

> So shall they fear the name of the Lord from the west, and his glory from the rising of the sun. When the enemy shall come in like a flood, the Spirit of the Lord shall lift up a standard against him.
> Isaiah 59:19

> For though we walk in the flesh, we do not war after the flesh: For the weapons of our warfare are not carnal (fleshy) but mighty through God to the pulling down of strongholds.
> 2 Corinthians 10:3-4

Who is the King of Glory? The Lord strong and mighty, the Lord mighty in battle. Children of God, we need not fight in this battle: set yourselves, stand, be still and know your God. He will be exalted in every battle.

I wondered about witchcraft for years. I asked how it was possible for someone to use witchcraft to inflict another person with physical maladies. How does it work? It works through spells, incantation, hexes and curses. All of these accomplish the same purpose – summoning a demon or demons to perform a given action. Frequently incantations are in poetic form and have been passed down from generation to generation. They are usually spoken aloud, but often are spoken by the witch spirit into the spirit world. The term placing a spell, hex or curse on someone refers to the act of calling up a demon and then sending it to the person to perform influences or damage.

Don't be mistaken, witches and wizards do have incredible power. The Sisters of Light, an organization in Satan's kingdom, first came to the United States from Europe in the late 1700s. They date back to the Dark Ages in Europe but indeed can trace their roots back to the sorcerers of ancient Egypt and Babylon.

They were powerful enough to be able to reproduce three of the ten plagues sent upon Egypt during Moses' time (see Exodus 7). They were able to produce disease and to kill without ever physically touching the victim, even from more than a thousand miles away; they were able to accomplish this through demons. They can inflict the body with many diseases that often cannot be diagnosed by a doctor.

Witches can astral-project their spirits into the spirit world and launch their attacks and influences. I read of a witch who said, "I don't have a formula for this manifestation, I only know I can do it because of the powerful entities that dwell in me." She also mentioned that because she refused to perform human and animal sacrifices, she had many illnesses, including cancer.

Luke 13:11-13 offers an account of a woman who had a spirit of infirmity for 18 years. She was in a bowed position and couldn't lift herself. Jesus saw her condition and loosed her from the spirit of infirmity. He laid His hands on her and immediately she was made straight and she glorified God. Her infirmity was caused by Satan, but please bear in mind that all infirmities cannot be uniformly blamed on the devil. The Bible, however, does enumerate several cases.

> And the Lord said unto Satan, behold he is in thine hand; but save his life. So went Satan from the presence of the Lord,

and smote Job with sore boils from the sole of his feet unto his crown.

Job 2:6-7

How God anointed Jesus of Nazareth with the Holy Ghost and with power: Who went about doing good, and healing all that were oppressed of the devil; For God was with him.

Acts 10:38

To deliver such an one unto Satan for the destruction of the flesh, that the spirit may be saved in the day of the Lord Jesus.

1 Corinthians 5:5

And lest I should be exalted above measure through the abundance of the revelations, there was given to me a thorn in the flesh, the messenger of Satan to buffet me, lest I should be exalted above measure.

2 Corinthians 12:7

Concerning operations in the spirit world, there are certain things the natural man will never grasp. It's downright foolishness. The wise are confused but praise God for spiritual insight about the forces of darkness.

But the natural man receiveth not the things of the Spirit of God: for they are foolishness unto him: neither can he know them, because they are spiritually discerned. But he that is spiritual judgeth all things, yet he himself is judged of no man.

I Corinthians 2:14-15

CHAPTER 8

Confounding the "Wise"

I recently read about a very interesting, yet frightening, phenomenon known as being bitten by demons. My first remarks were, "Please! What is this?" But in the twinkling of an eye I remembered my leg and what it was that could have stung me.

In the story a city jail inmate puzzled police and medical examiners with her tale about demons biting her. This young girl claimed she was bitten twenty times and she shouted when she was hurt.

She was questioned by a crowd of observers then suddenly her facial expressions changed to anguish and terror as if she were confronted by "The Thing." She looked around wildly and then screamed and struggled, hit her arms and shoulders, then her strenuous resistance ceased. She collapsed into the arms of those holding her, weak and half conscious.

She was bitten on the right knee and other bite marks appeared on her neck, arms and shoulders. Observers insisted that they were within sight of her at all times. The chief of police said that it was a realistic example of a horrified woman being bitten to insanity by invisible persons. An onlooker witnessed her being bitten three times.

She screamed and with her eyes flashing fire, she pointed to the parts of her body being attacked, then she fell almost senseless into the hands of those standing by. She pointed to teeth marks with saliva surrounding them.

We cannot understand why we are afflicted at times, but sometimes the affliction is working for our own good. Our light affliction cannot be compared to the glory that's to be revealed. This is the word the apostle Paul wrote to the people of Corinth to encourage them. The scripture states in 2 Corinthians 4:17; for our light affliction, which is but for a moment, worketh for us a far more exceeding and eternal weight of glory.

During this girl's ordeal, a man of God was listening to the radio when the disc jockey exclaimed, ladies and gentlemen, if you have a weak heart, please sit down or turn your radio off. For some unknown reason this statement grabbed the attention of the man of God as he listened.

Prior to our ordeals God provides a way of escape. His Word says He will not give us more than we can bear. This is a nugget of truth written in 1 Corinthians 10:13; There hath no temptation taken you but such as common to man: but God is faithful who will not suffer you to be tempted above that ye are able; but will with the temptation also make a way of escape, that ye may be able to bear it.

This chosen man of God was knowledgeable and called for the ministry of deliverance. He heard screams followed by pandemonium. Doctors said the girl's actions could be explained. They said their records showed that this was epilepsy – an extreme hysteria.

The man of God could hear someone saying, "Look, the marks of teeth are appearing." Another said, "The girl is being choked by some unseen thing. She is blue in the face and there are marks on her neck." Then the girl screamed again.

This chosen deliverer said to his wife, "This girl isn't sick and these people are helpless before the devil." He then began to talk to His heavenly Father. God's people are not to be anxious about anything. Everything must be taken to Him in prayer.

Philippians 4:6-7; be not careful for nothing: but in everything by prayer and supplication with thanksgiving let your requests be made known unto God. And the peace of God, which passeth all understanding, shall keep your hearts and minds through Christ Jesus. He prayed for God to deliver this girl but God's response to him was to tell him that he would only deliver the girl if he went personally to her.

There are times when we are fervent in prayer for the need of others but fear binds us and we often complain of inadequacies or imperfections. This man of God could have prayed where he was and God may have delivered the girl just as He did for the man in the Bible who said to Jesus, "Just speak the word and my son shall be healed."

There is no doubt that God wants to be glorified amidst these educated professors, lecturers and onlookers who say there is no God and who have no understanding of the kingdom of darkness. This was no fairytale and many tried to help this unfortunate young lady but failed. This was going to be a real battle between God and the one who comes to steal, kill and destroy mankind. After much prayer and assurance that God wanted him to go to the girl, the man of God sought permission from the police and medical authorities to see her.

The head of the medical unit had been working in the field of medicine for 38 years and had performed 8,000 autopsies yet he had never accepted the theory of non-material forces existing in the universe. This professor wasn't interested in the girl's affairs. To him it was nonsense but one day he bumped into her.

He first noticed the reddish human-like bite impressions on her arms and was convinced that this girl had bitten herself. They considered her abnormal and agreed to recommend her for treatment in the National Psychopathic Hospital.

Upon reading this account I was moved with compassion, for many people have been considered abnormal because the problem cannot be diagnosed by a doctor. Such persons are sometimes confined to some kind of mental institution without any hope of recovery or release. This is quite sad, for indeed some of these infirmities or physical maladies can be attributed to the demonic.

I pray earnestly to God that we will become equipped to loose people from such bondage. The church is designed by God for the works of the ministry, the perfecting of the saints for the edifying of the body of Christ (see Ephesians 4:11-12).

Later, visitors wanted to hear the professor's opinion of this girl so they brought in the unconscious girl for examination. The man of God was among them and he scrutinized carefully the exposed parts of her body to find out whether they had bite impressions.

Weak and unable to stand alone, the girl had to be helped by someone who placed her on a bed. In a semi-trance she screamed loudly, and clear marks or impressions of human-like teeth marks from both the upper and lower jaws were very evident. The area was moist and the teeth impressions were those of the front or incisor teeth.

No one could understand how the bites were produced since the girl's hands had been held away from her mouth. It could not have been the person who held her because he didn't have a single tooth in his head, having recently had them all extracted.

The girl continued to scream, fell into a trance, then awoke and began to speak intelligently. She said she'd been bitten by two very black and ugly human-like fellows. This was a very unusual and frightening incident and the professor said, "I must admit I'm afraid."

If I had been in his situation, I would not have to be told to run for my life, because this situation was beyond comprehension. Someone would have to be bold and empowered by the Holy Ghost to stand flat-footed and address that which seemed to be invisible.

Peter addressed Elymas the great magician when he was offered money for the power of God, he said to the sorcerer, "May you and your money perish, for the gift of God cannot be purchased with money."

A girl with the spirit of divination followed Paul around for days and announced that Paul and Silas would show everyone the way to salvation. Paul, empowered by the Holy Ghost, commanded the spirit to come out of this girl and it came out of her the same hour. This spirit of divination in this poor girl brought great wealth for these people so when the means of living was extinguished they sought to kill these vessels of honor.

God anointed Jesus of Nazareth with the Holy Ghost and power and Jesus confronted the madman of Gadara, asked the demons for their names and cast them out. We have to know who we are in Christ and with confidence know that we have authority over the powers of the devil.

The man of God, whom God chose to help this possessed girl, seized the moment to convince the professor that demons existed. He told the professor that there are only three powers in the universe: the positive power (or the power of a creative and benevolent God); the human power (or the power of men on earth); and the negative power (or the malevolent and sinister power of the devil). First he asked the professor if he thought the girl was acting under God's power: The professor shook his head slowly and said, "No not God's power." Next he asked him, given his experience with human beings, if he felt she was acting like a human being.

The professor responded, "No, the actions of this girl are not related to human beings." The professor was then told that there was only one power left and that was the demonic power. Therefore this girl must be acting under demonic power. The professor admitted that his experiences hadn't prepared him for encounters with something that was beyond a doubt supernatural.

Then this great man of God who stood in the gap for this girl said, "If this girl has demon power in her, Jesus Christ can deliver her from that power." He then turned to Mark 16:17 and read: "And these signs shall follow them that believe; In My name shall they cast out devils; they shall speak with new tongues." He then asked the professor if he believed this.

The professor looked at him and said, "I believe, but who will help us? Everyone has refused to pray for her."

The man of God said, "I will pray for her, but without any kind of medication given to her. If Jesus heals her, all the glory must be given to Him."

God will always watch over his word to perform it. Jesus said, "The spirit of the Lord is upon me; because the Lord hath anointed me to preach good tidings unto the meek; He hath sent me to bind up the broken-hearted, to proclaim liberty to the captives, and the opening of the prison to them that are bound" (Isaiah 61:1).

In Luke 4:18; Jesus took the scroll and read about Himself, "the Spirit of the Lord is upon Me, because He has chosen Me to bring good news to the poor. He has sent Me to proclaim liberty to the captive and recovery of sight to the blind; to set free the oppressed."

In Matthew 4:23-24 it states, "Jesus went about all Galilee, teaching in their synagogues, and preaching the gospel of the kingdom, and healing all manner of sickness and all manner of disease among the people. And His fame went throughout all Syria: and they brought unto Him all sick people that were taken with divers diseases and torments, and those that were oppressed with devils, and those which were lunatic, and those that had the palsy;

and they were healed. It doesn't matter how bound you are, Jesus can set you free. He whom the Son sets free is free indeed.

Now a remarkable deliverance service was about to take place. The heathens and skeptics were about to have a difference of opinion concerning our sovereign God. There was a huge gathering. Many had already seen the teeth marks on the girl and had observed the failure of the doctors, psychiatrists and spiritualists. They had never heard prayer for the diseased and demon-possessed.

As they brought the girl in she looked keenly at each person but when her eyes caught a glimpse of God's anointed vessel her eyes widened and she glared at him. "I don't like you!" she exclaimed.

The demons knew their time had come to be disengaged from their comfort zone. The residence they took by force was about to be inhabited by the anointed one and His anointing. The demons used her lips to curse God and this man of God. She was called by her name and told that she would be delivered from the devils through the all-powerful name of Jesus for there is no other name by which man can be saved.

> "Wherefore God also hath highly exalted him, and given him a name which is above every name: That at the name of Jesus every knee should bow, of things in heaven, and things in earth, and things under the earth. And that every tongue should confess that Jesus Christ is Lord, to the glory of God the Father."
>
> Philippians 2:9-11

> Neither is there salvation in any other: for there is none other name under heaven given among men, whereby we can be saved.
>
> Acts 4:12

The spirit of fear gripped this young girl as she began to scream and begged this soldier of Jesus Christ to leave her alone." They will kill me," she said. Then she showed him the teeth marks, some of which were very severe. Others were bleeding and still others showed broken blood vessels below the surface of the skin.

This was the greatest battle of this man's life and the war began. God was in control but the girl was not delivered the same day. God started a work and the man of God was instructed to fast and go back to the girl. Then she would be delivered.

> And he said unto them, this kind can come forth by nothing, but prayer and fasting.
>
> Mark 9:29

> Is not this the fast that I have chosen? To loose the bands of wickedness, to undo the heavy burdens, and to let the oppressed go free, and that he break every yoke.
>
> Isaiah 58:6

He invited another man of faith to accompany him the next day and God moved by His Spirit.

> Again I say unto you, that if two of you shall agree on earth as touching anything that they shall ask, it shall be done for them of my Father which is in heaven. For where two or three are gathered together in my name, there am I in the midst of them.
>
> Matthew 18:19-20

The demons were confronted and commanded by a man of God endowed with the Holy Spirit and power and therefore these devils couldn't resist him. They had to loose their hold. They fled and haven't returned nor has the girl been bitten since. Glory be to God! He is worthy to be praised.

This incident had such a great impact on those who gathered to see what was going to happen that tears could been seen running down the faces of many. They knew something wonderful had happened by a power that supersedes the evil power of darkness. This young girl's case couldn't be solved by medical or psychological science. She was delivered by the power of simple prayer to Christ. A Christian and married, this girl now experiences wholeness in her body, soul and spirit and is a witness to many that Christ is our savior. The glory and praise for this miracle belong to God and His Son, Jesus Christ.

There is absolutely no need for anyone to doubt the above account. Satan desires to sift God's children as wheat but God will not allow him to. He is a defeated foe and that's why we ought not to give him a foothold in our lives.

CHAPTER 9

Evidences of the Demonic

The Bible relates the story of a little boy with a dumb spirit whom the devil tried to destroy.

> And one of the multitude answered and said, Master, I have brought unto thee my son, which has a dumb spirit; And wheresoever he taketh him, he teareth him; And he foameth, and gnasheth with His teeth, and pineth away: and I spake to thy disciples that they should cast him out but they could not. He answereth him, and sayeth, oh faithless generation, how long shall I be with you? How long shall I suffer you, bring him unto me.
>
> Mark 9:17-29

When the spirit saw Jesus, it immediately threw the boy into convulsions. He fell to the ground and rolled around, foaming at the mouth. Jesus asked the boy's father how long he had been like this. The father said from childhood; the boy was often thrown into fire or water to kill him.

There was a desperate cry for help to the one who is a present help in the time of trouble. Psalm 46:1; God is our refuge and strength, a very present help in trouble. He is able to do exceeding abundantly more than we can ask or think because of the power that is at work in us.

Jesus came to set free those who are oppressed by devils. He has never lost a battle. Jesus resisted the devil and triumphed over him during His wilderness experience. Many devils or unclean spirits cried out, fleeing from their place of residence when confronted by Him.

Jesus gave the boy's father words of comfort: "All things are possible to him that believeth."

The boy's father exclaimed, "I do believe, help me overcome my unbelief."

Then Jesus rebuked the evil spirit, "Thou dumb and deaf spirit, I charge thee, come out of him, and enter no more into him."

The spirit shrieked, caused the boy to convulse violently, and came out. The boy looked so much like a corpse that many said, "He's dead." But Jesus took him by the hand and lifted him to His feet. And he stood up.

We must charge or cast out demons in the name of Jesus. Jesus did so with the finger of God and none resisted him. He said to the woman that was bowed down for eighteen years, you are loosed from your infirmity. He laid his hands on her and immediately she was made straight, and glorified God.

When the chains or fetters are broken praise is what the victor should do. The anointed King David said, praise must continually be in our mouths. It is the fruit of our lips giving thanks to His name.

Satan and His demons desire to inhabit and afflict man's body, soul and spirit. Owing to the fact that the body is the temple of the Holy Ghost, Satan should have no legal right to God's vessel. On the contrary, there are often gateways or doorways left open for him to gain entry.

I was not a Christian when I was afflicted by demons. In my own right I had no defense against demons. The fact is, I escaped death only because my mother interceded for me and God would not allow me to die because He had a purpose for my life.

Glory be to God! Let me say this to you: it does not matter what happens to you in life. If God's plan in heaven is for you to be a chosen vessel in the earth, He is faithful to bring this to pass. So even if you are encountering countless complex situations, He is working in your favor.

Our sufferings presently cannot be compared to the glory that is to be revealed. Romans 8:18; for I reckon that the sufferings of this present time are not worthy to be compared with the glory which shall be revealed in us.

When you are suffering it is very hard to say rejoice in hope, be patient in affliction and faithful in prayer. How can you be faithful in prayer when you are sorely afflicted? King Jesus was, and His example is for our learning.

In Hebrews 5:7, the Word of the Lord says, "Who in the days of His flesh, when He had offered up prayers and supplications with strong crying and tears unto Him that was able to save Him from death, and was heard in that He feared."

How did I get a swollen leg? I could have been touched directly or indirectly by demonic forces. My dad's leg was affected and swelled up like mine, and my mom had to take authority over hers. The things that we cannot see and know can be devastating if God does not intervene. The Omniscient one sees the net, the trap, the chain or fetter that so easily beset us. Nothing is too hard for God. Jeremiah 32:17, 27; Ah Lord God! Behold, thou hast made the heaven and the earth by thy great power and stretched out arm, and there is nothing too hard for thee. Behold, I am the Lord, the God of all flesh, is there any thing too hard for me?

Possessed Possessions

There are many people (Christians included) who like collectibles, as I do. I have never thought about their origin or the purpose of their production. Many Christians possess and use articles of evil in all aspects of life. These items can be very devastating when worn or displayed as objects of art in our homes. There are times when we cannot explain why we have certain odd sensations or we cannot figure out certain things.

Certain dolls of Africa, religious figurines, or implements of ritual and voodoo are things we unknowingly embrace, to our detriment. Some of these articles contain spirits that have possessed them throughout history, have never left them, and are just as strong today as they were in the past.

I have often heard of people who bought souvenirs, symbolic stones and other memorabilia not knowing that along with those objects, the devil has been invited into their homes permanently.

A story is told of a family who bought a seemingly harmless souvenir box that eventually affected every member of the household adversely. The family kept this gift for a number of years not knowing what the content of the box was. Made of bamboo, the box had colorful markings made from berry dye. When they opened the box, six tiny human figurines constructed from a thin brown fiber toppled out upon one another. These little men had markings to indicate eyes and hair.

There's no doubt these were satanic voodoo dolls. A note inside the box related the whole story of their spirit meaning and purpose. Here is the history, power and mystery of these six little men in a tiny box: There were six members in the family and each had a specific demon. According to a specialist on things of the occult, the spirits of these figurines in such boxes control the inhabitants of the house where they dwell through dreams and the imagination. If they didn't use these little men in bamboo boxes, symbolic animals, such as the bird, the cat and the dog were used.

Each of these animal spirits had a specific mission and purpose to affect an individual's life. According to a book of enchantments owned by the specialist, the bird spirit was represented by the wind and was meant to induce a certain sensation which was quite eerie. The cat spirit, on the other hand, brought trouble. Finally, the dog spirit brought protection to a person's life. Whenever these little dolls were taken out of the box or the lid was lifted off, the spirits were released into the house to work their demonic magic.

For 13 long years this family was severely affected by these demonic dolls but knew nothing about them. So many innocent people are destroyed because of lack of knowledge. Wisdom is the principal thing and we ought to get wisdom accompanied by understanding. Wisdom is knowledge with the ability to use it.

> Wisdom is the principal thing; therefore get wisdom: and with all thy getting get understanding.
>
> Proverbs 4:7

These dolls caused devastation in this family. They were unable to stay in one place of residence for more than a year at a time.

During a nine-year period, the family moved twelve times. They experienced financial instability and were never able to break free from the spirit of poverty.

The most unusual thing that happened, however, was an unnatural swelling of each member's left ankle. This information struck a chord with me, though it's not always easy to determine where the evil influence in the life of an individual originates.

As I mentioned, before His death my father suffered a swollen left leg and my mother had to pray for hers. I have struggled with mine for years and have seen 15 outstanding specialists in the city of Toronto. Not one has been able to diagnose what caused my leg to swell. I decided on numerous occasions never to see another podiatrist but to pray for my leg.

I've had creeping sensations in this leg. It never hurts but feels as if I'm dragging a thousand pounds of lead at times. I know without a shadow of a doubt that it is a result of demonic activity. When I fast, my leg is not swollen. This baffled me for years.

So many people had prayed for my leg but no one was able to command this spirit to loose its hold. I remember one night I went to church and my leg was very swollen. I asked the pastor to pray for me. This is a night I will never forget.

The pastor proceeded to pray and lay her hand on my leg and the demon was very disturbed. The hand which the pastor used to hold my leg was attacked. Within a twinkling of an eye her hand was swollen and her sleeve burst wide open.

Everyone was in shock and some people were scared to come near me. As a matter of fact, a lady passed by when the pastor was ministering to me and said, "In the name of Jesus." Then something grabbed her leg. She was very frightened because she had never had such an experience.

As Christians we should trust the Lord with all our hearts and if we lean not on our own understanding, He will give us the spirit of discernment to distinguish a spiritual situation from a natural one.

Many have died because of ignorance or lack of knowledge. Hosea 4:6 says, "My people are destroyed for lack of knowledge: because you have rejected knowledge." Oh, may the eyes of our understanding be enlightened so that we may not be defeated!

> The eyes of your understanding being enlightened; that ye may know what is the hope of his calling, and what the riches of the glory of his inheritance in the saints. And what is the exceeding greatness of his power to us-ward who believe, according to the working of his mighty power. Which he wrought in Christ, when he raised him from the dead, and set him at his own right hand in the heavenly places. For above all principality, and power, and might, and dominion, and every name that is named, not only in this world, but also in that which is to come: And hath put all things under his feet, and gave him to be head over all things to the church? Which is his body, the fullness of him that filleth all in all?
> Ephesians 1:18-23

Satan destroys mankind in stages. His desire is to kill, steal and destroy God's created beings, mankind. We are instructed to be sober and vigilant, because our adversary, the devil, as a roaring lion, walketh about, seeking whom he may devour.

> Be sober, be vigilant, because your adversary the devil, as a roaring lion, walketh about, seeking whom he may devour. Whom resist steadfast in the faith, knowing that the same afflictions are accompanied in your brethren that are in the world. But the God of all grace, who hath called us unto his eternal glory by Christ Jesus, after that ye have suffered a while, make you perfect, stablish, strengthen, settle you.
> 1 Peter 5:8-10

CHAPTER 10

Demonic Possession

The devil seldom takes a life all at once. The devil attacks and eats away at the mind, especially those minds that are not on him. We must remember that we have the mind of Christ and it is to be gird with truth; Philippians 2:5; let this mind be in you, which was also in Christ Jesus. Such a mind cannot be controlled by demonic powers. We are admonished to wear our spiritual armor, including the helmet of salvation.

The devil devours the human personality bit by bit. He's like a cancer. At certain stages of demonic interferences a person can be saved. Therefore, it's of great importance to know the steps he uses to destroy human life; let us not shrink back and be destroyed.

Evangelist Lester Sumrall, in his book entitled, "Demons the answer book" said, there are seven steps toward full demonic possession. The steps to possession follow a logical order to a final conclusion. The steps begin with the smallest amount of demon power that hurts a person and continues until the person is completely overwhelmed.

We must understand how the devil attacks and harasses the human personality. As children of the Most High God, we must be confident that Jesus Christ has come to set us free from anything the devil tries to do. The devil is no threat to our Advocate, the Light of our salvation and Good Shepherd.

Jesus laid down His life for us and is now resurrected and is seated at the right hand of His Father pleading for us. The Word of the Lord declares in 1John 3:8 that it was for this purpose the Son of man was manifested that He might destroy the work of the devil.

The accuser of the brethren and the destroyer of man, a Tripartite (spirit, soul and body), hates God's sons and daughters and his aim is to destroy God's people. Look at what the Word of the Lord says in John 10:10: the thief comes not but to steal, and kill and destroy.

But God will encompass His people with songs of deliverance, and mercy shall encompass them about. Our hedge of protection will be around us. We must overcome the devil by the blood of the Lamb and the Word of His testimony.

The right hand of God the Father is a figurative expression symbolizing the Almighty God's power, authority and glory. How awesome is it to know that our names are engraved in the palm of His hand. No powers of darkness can pluck us out of His righteous right hand. His Word declares that His hand will lead us and His right hand will hold us. His hand is not shortened so that he cannot save His people who are called by His name. (Isaiah 59:1)

It's very important to analyze the devil's steps. If we can identify with any of the following in our lives, then we should not be dismayed for Jesus is able to do for us what no other power can. The Word of the Lord declares that He is able to do exceedingly abundantly more than we can ask or think because of His mighty power, which works in us.

Step 1: Regression

Regression is the first of the devil's attacks on one's personality. It is a battle against a person's God-given abilities of release and expression. To regress in the human personality is to go backward in spiritual force and power.

We are all created to progress and advance. When this goes into reverse, all the negative forces are at work and, in fact, signs of the first step are at times very evident around us, predominantly in our homes and churches.

A person who is articulate and sociable might be seen at times to be antisocial or dysfunctional. A person might be excited about moving forward and may make the necessary plans to do so but then procrastinates. Such a person can be very listless and tend not to care about what happens around him or her.

The accuser of the brethren works like this. He first binds his victim with a light cord of regression. At this stage if he or she is alert and knows that the enemy is at work he or she can snap his bonds and be free. Jesus came to set us free, and we will be free indeed. God's children will have the victory over the enemy for it is He who will trample that old dragon.

> Through God we shall do valiantly: for He it is that shall tread down our enemies.
> Psalm 60:12

If we submit to the Almighty and resist the devil, he will have to take up his weapons and flee. We have to confront him and say to him, "It is written." Then he will have to loose his hold on his victim. Don't stay bound and let him add stronger bonds so as to keep you trapped and enslaved. Be God's soldier of the cross and be ready to march and take authority over the devil's power and set the captives free.

When the enemy comes in like a flood, the Spirit of God will take up a standard. He will be our defense. Do not be afraid. God has not given us the spirit of fear but of power, love and a sound mind.

> For God hath not given us the spirit of fear; but of power, and of love, and of a sound mind.
> 2 Timothy 1:7

Step 2: Repression

To repress is to restrain from without; to repress a person is to destroy the natural expression God gives at birth. To repress a personality is to take the joy and gladness out of that life. God did not create human lives to be restrained by an abnormal environment.

It is interesting to note that God makes every human an expressionist. After delivery of a newborn baby, the doctor needs to hear the baby cry. If that doesn't happen he suspects that the baby may be dead. Sad to say, many of God's people are like dead people.

They prefer to give you the silent treatment or they will just mutter under their breath. If a person's inner feelings are repressed he can be considered a dead person.

It's also interesting to note that God desires exuberant expression from us, and this can be shown in our eyes. The eyes are the mirrors of the soul. There are those who will walk with their eyes in a fixed gaze. This reveals bondage of the soul. Our face should be radiant, shining forth the glory of the Lord. Wearing a frown can make a person very unapproachable. To lose the spirit of joy and happiness is to take the road to a ruined personality. Joy is one fruit of the Holy Spirit and many Christians have never experienced the joy of salvation. The joy of the Lord is our strength. Let us purpose in our hearts to fix our eyes upon the Lord when we are overwhelmed by the forces of darkness.

Here is a typical example of a person who is repressed. Away from God's house a repressed person is pleasant and talkative. Upon reaching the property of the sanctuary something suddenly happens to this person. There is a frown on the face, the body becomes stiff and the eyes are fixed in a glare. There is no invitation to socialize and the signal is to stay away; the person is not interested.

This person will walk into church and sit quietly, not interacting with anyone. He or she remains expressionless for the whole church service. If we cannot enter into fellowship with others, how can we enter into fellowship with Jesus? Our body is the temple of the Holy Spirit. He dwells in us and He has to glorify Himself in our vessels. Therefore, if the body remains rigid and expressionless, it means the body, soul and spirit are bound and deliverance is needed.

The Word of the Lord declares that we should serve God with all our strength, soul and spirit. God's children need to know that they're not meant to be bound but free. So, we need to be an expression of praise. We can praise Him by opening our mouths and singing songs unto Him, clapping our hands, raising our arms, stamping our feet, dancing and making a joyful noise.

When our body, soul and spirit are sanctified unto the Father, He will use us for His glory. Watch the person who's bound as soon as church is dismissed, or even before the benediction is pronounced. You can read the body language, he or she is uneasy and tries to get away as quickly as possible. Away from the church this person becomes jovial again. This is a repressed person who needs help.

Any one can be a repressor. The repressor will react in such a way that everybody's attention will be attracted. A parent can cause misery or unhappiness and a teacher can cause a student to be sad and nervous.

The devil is the cause of these reactions and we need to resist him. His desire is to steal our joy which is our strength. Therefore, brethren, let's be careful that we are not repressing each other, but rather let every man be an expressionist according to the will of God.

Step 3: Suppression

The third step is suppression or an abnormal squeezing down, crushing or concealing, as to suppress information. Suppression deteriorates our emotions and destroys our personal happiness. Suppression comes from without and hinders us from expressing our feelings. When feelings are not expressed we know for sure that this is not of God.

Suppressed people are very weak and are not excited by anything. They are very negative and have a "don't care" attitude. One may be suppressed at times, but not all the time. There are times we have to speak to the soul like David did.

> Why art thou cast down, O my soul? And why art thou disquieted in me? Hope thou in God: For I shall yet praise him for the help of his countenance.
> Psalm 42:5

When we are too afraid to encourage ourselves, or there is no interest to do so a word of comfort from a friend is so soothing at times. Good words motivate you to hang in there a little longer, not to mention when a friend mentions your name in prayer. As children of the Most High God, we must purpose in our hearts to pray without ceasing and to do so with supplication in the Spirit, watching with perseverance, praying for all God's people.

When we pray God will deliver and He will cause war to cease. Psalm 46:9; He maketh wars to cease unto the end of the earth; he breaketh the bow and cutteth the spear in sunder; he burneth the chariot in the fire. God is able to cause war to cease in the mind and He will use our mind for His glory. Amen.

Step 4: Depression

Depression is a broken spirit. A person is pressed down until his spirit is crushed. God does not want anyone to be depressed and sad. If our eyes are taken off Him and we become anxious about our situations a depressing spirit will enter the doorway of our lives. God's Word says we are to rejoice. Sometimes, we can be depressed but not for an extended period of time.

Depression is no respecter of persons. David a man after God's own heart had adverse situations in his life, as he lived as an anointed king yet a fugitive. He had to encourage himself. He asked himself why he was downcast and why his spirit was so disturbed within him. He told himself to put his hope in God, and praise Him.

Then once when he was overwhelmed, he began to cry out to the Lord.

> Hear my cry, o God; attend unto my prayer. From the end of the earth will I cry unto thee, when my heart is overwhelmed: lead me to the rock that is higher than I. For thou hast been a shelter for me, and a strong tower from the enemy.
> Psalm 61:1-3

We ought to remember that the name of the Lord is a strong tower the righteous run into Him and they are safe. The devil prowls around to take advantage of people and he does cause confusion that will destroy their happiness, home and sometimes their life through suicide. Many times depression is triggered by loss or serious trouble, heavy financial burdens, family problems or disappointment.

A beautiful Christian lady migrated from one of the Caribbean Islands to North America, when she became a citizen; she went home and married her high school boyfriend. After two years he joined his lovely wife and what should have been a happy union was a troublesome relationship. They did not communicate and this caused great confusion and stress in their relationship.

She would fight him like a man and he would treat her like a punching bag. She said many times that she was going to kill him. They sought counselling but no one succeeded in ministering to them.

She got so overwhelmed one day that she decided to take her life. So she packed up her stuff, got undressed, and began to walk down the middle of a busy street. People were astonished, they could not believe what they saw. Someone who was very concerned called the police and they took her to the hospital where they assessed her and determined that she was depressed. They gave her antidepressants but she got worse. But thank God, this was not her fate for the word of the Lord declares that He has a plan to prosper us and not to harm us.

The prayer of faith will cause those who are bound to be delivered. A few prayer warriors gathered together and prayed for her and God was faithful. He answered the prayer of faith and delivered her.

Take a look at these scriptures in 1 John chapter 5:14-15; And this is the confidence that we have in him that, if we ask any thing according to his will, he heareth us. And if we know that he hear us, whatsoever we ask we know that we have the petitions that we desired of him.

He will bring every man and woman to their expected end for we know in whom we believe and He is able to keep us against that day. If we are caught between a rock and hard place, God is able to see us through.

Depression is dangerous because it often brings about an abnormal state of inactivity. People may sit staring into space, hearing nothing, saying nothing and doing nothing. Depressed people feel a sadness too deep to express and too painful to cry about. They have reached a point where they make no effort to try. They have lost hope. But our hope should be built on nothing less than Jesus' blood and righteousness. We dare not trust the sweetest frame but only lean on Jesus' name.

If you're depressed constantly, deliverance is needed. Only Jesus can provide the cure for depression. Call upon Christ and place all your problems, heartaches and worries in His keeping, casting all your cares upon Him, for He cares for you.

Be encouraged and say with the apostle Paul, "For the which cause also suffer these things: nevertheless I'm not ashamed: for I know whom I have believed, and I am persuaded that He is able to keep that which I have committed unto him against that day" (2 Timothy 1:12).

Rebuke the devil when he tries to weigh you down with sadness and perplexity. Say to him, "I'm trusting in God, and I don't have to be worried or anxious or sad or depressed. Loose your hold, Satan, in Jesus' name." A frown or downcast face won't resolve your problems, only Jesus can. Begin to bless the Lord as David did in Psalm 103:11, "Bless the Lord, O my soul: and all that is within me bless His holy name."

Step 5: Oppression

Oppression is the weighing down of someone with something he or she is not able to carry. The children of Israel were oppressed in Egypt. They were treated cruelly, beaten unmercifully and crushed down until they were not able to carry their burden. They cried out to God earnestly and He sent them a deliverer. Oh, that we would cry out to God when we are oppressed, for He will surely deliver us!

God knew His children would be oppressed, therefore, He sent Jesus – the One who sets His people free. Acts 10:38 tells us that God anointed Jesus to heal all who were oppressed of the devil.

There are many people who are oppressed by fear. God hasn't given the spirit of fear to us, but power and strong minds. The mind is Satan's battleground where he deceives mankind. The devil wants us to worry until we have no use for ourselves. We must resist him, knowing that we do have the mind of Christ. A Christ-minded person will not allow a spirit of depression to have him or her bound.

Satan is a liar and the father of all lies. He wants God's people to be slaves of oppression but let us not succumb to him. Let's tell him, "It is written God will keep my mind in perfect peace because I will endeavor to fix my eyes upon Him."

Satan, the prince of this world, is one who tries many ways to crush our spirit by way of insensitive, so-called friends, disaster and trouble. He may rush as a flood and overwhelm you with demonic power that causes you to be battered and bruised on every side, but God is not far away.

David prayed when he was overwhelmed.

> Hear my cry, O God; attend unto my prayer. From the end of the earth will I cry unto thee, when my heart is overwhelmed: lead me to the rock that is higher than I.
>
> Psalm 61:1-2

This rock is Jesus, the only one, be very sure. Be very sure, our anchor holds and grips the solid rock. Jesus is our rock in a weary land of oppression, a shelter in the time of storm. The time of storm is what makes us victims of oppression but we must know how to trust and obey our Maker. Oppression can be overcome by taking authority over the devil through the all-powerful name of Jesus.

Step 6: Obsession

Obsession is an act of an evil spirit in besetting a person or impelling him to unreasonable action. Webster's dictionary says obsession is complete domination of the mind by one idea, a fixed idea; obsession can come by believing a lie through jealousy and hatred.

A relationship can be ruined because of the spirit of jealousy, as the man and woman may not trust the relationship shared, and as a result, there's no peace of mind when they are away from each other. As a result of this mistrust it creates doubt and fear whereby thinking that the possibility might exist where one can become unfaithful.

There is life in the Word of God, and when we rightly divide the Word then the spirit of obsession will not enslave us. This will give us the confidence we need. Tell it to Jesus. He's a friend even if no other friend can be found. Talk to a minister or believer of the gospel of Jesus Christ who is filled with the Holy Spirit. God has endowed His servant or vessel of honor with power for service and nothing is impossible to them who believe. God will do exceedingly and abundantly more that we can ask or think.

An obsessed person has no willpower and is weak and helpless before the devil. Do not shrink back and be destroyed, pick yourself up, brush yourself off and call out to Him, while He may be found and while He's near. He will answer you and help you.

Get to the right person for help—a man or woman of faith, full of the Holy Spirit and fire. He or she will be able to knock on heaven's door, and surely the one who made the heavens will rend them. God will do the miraculous – what a mighty God we serve! Lord, let there be vessels of honor to show forth the power that is of God and not of ourselves.

Step 7: Possession

It is not only possible for Satan to subject people to himself, but he can also take actual possession of them. Possession is usually just a further development of demonic subjection. The demon-possessed person is under the absolute, total control of the devil. The devil is now capable of controlling the mind and is the master of that person's thinking and doing. Many people in this position are led to do abominable things they wouldn't have done if they were in their right mind. They are helpless in the hands of a diabolical monster.

Possession can also occur at the death of an already possessed person, whose evil spirit leaves and enters an unbelieving descendent. Many people who are prepared to believe in the existence of demonic subjection will deny the possibility of possession, yet the scriptures themselves recognize both these forms of the demonic and distinguish clearly between them.

For example we read in John 13:2 that the devil put it into the heart of Judas Iscariot to betray Jesus, and later in the same chapter in verse 27, we find, "Then after the sop, Satan entered into him (Judas)." During the time of Christ and the apostles possessed people actually did exist.

Furthermore, Jesus' statement in Mark 16:17 ("And these signs will follow them that believe; in my name shall they cast out devils") confirms that possession is still a phenomenon with which we have to deal today.

We must be careful to not confuse a severe case of demonic subjection with the effects of a mental illness or a so-called possession. There are times when the spirit of discernment is not operable; people do not minister to others the way they should and people are at times offended. I have seen this confusion many times and often times we are defeated because we do not know.

What are the actual symptoms of possession? Since demonic subjection very often merges almost imperceptibly into possession, the symptoms of the latter have much in common with the characteristics of demonic subjection. Therefore, it is sometimes difficult to distinguish between the two conditions.

Demon-possession is frequently accompanied by additional symptoms of screaming, cursing, raving, grinding of teeth and violence. A possessed person may cause damage to objects or cause self-injury in an attempt to take his or her own life.

Occasionally a possessed person will emit a scornful laugh if he hears someone talking about Jesus, the cross of Christ or the blood of Jesus. At other times he may see dark figures in the room. However, the demons themselves seldom speak out of a possessed person, since their desire is to remain unnoticed for as long as possible.

A spirit possessing the human body will use the person's voice to speak. This is quite frightening. I remember going to prayer meeting with my mom and someone spoke with a thunderous voice saying, "I am not afraid of that man!" He was referring to a gentle man attending the prayer meeting.

There are also one or two other remarkable, yet relatively infrequent, phenomena associated with possession. One of these is a trance-like state into which the possessed person may fall when a voice (not his own) speaks out of him in a language or languages he has never learned. On regaining consciousness he will remember nothing of what just happened.

Secondly, the possessed person sometimes exhibits extraordinary physical strength, a state of rage so strong that he must be physically restrained. Legion, the demon of Gadara written about in Mark 5, is an example of such activity.

Thirdly, the demon-possessed person may exhibit the power of clairvoyance that enables him to make statements about things that, humanly speaking, he would never have known. Such a person may, for example, just look at someone and perceive their character and the sins they have committed and accurately forecast what the future holds for them. Such statements will prove to be true as is illustrated in the case of the young girl who followed Paul and Silas in Philippi.

> And it came to pass, as we went to prayer, a certain damsel possessed with a spirit of divination met us, which brought her masters much gain by soothsaying. The same followed Paul and us, and cried, saying, these men are the servants of the Most High God, which shew unto us the way to salvation.
>
> Acts 16:16-17

It must be immediately pointed out, however, that clairvoyance does not only occur in cases of possession, but it is a faculty possessed by many other people. Although it is considered to be a gift by some, the majority recognize it to be a serious burden in their lives.

Another characteristic that occurs frequently is the observance of strange noises, footsteps and loud knocks in the vicinity of the possessed person at night. There are certain physical symptoms that occur in connection with demon-possession. The devil may try to torment his victim by causing him to suffer pain in different parts of the body. Pains afflict the body and cannot be attributed to any known diseases. This is the reason why some people visit the doctor quite frequently with the same complaint but no diagnosis. I do believe that a spiritual problem cannot be medically treated. We should not be ignorant but know what is at work in our lives and take the necessary measures to be safe.

Demon-possession sometimes reveals itself in forms of insanity, both temporary and permanent. Doctors who work in institutions or asylums know that a patient's mind may be clear at one time and at another time the person becomes like an animal. This is the coming and going of demonic power within the person.

CHAPTER 11

Demons and Disease

It's important to understand the difference between disease and sickness. A disease is a malady or ailment, or an unhealthy condition of the mind or body. It is a wasting away. Sickness is illness or physical or mental disorder. All disease and sickness can be made obedient to the Word of God because there is power and authority in His Word.

> And these signs shall follow them that believe; in my name shall they cast out devils; they shall speak with new tongues; they shall take up serpents; and if they drink any deadly thing, it shall not hurt them; they shall lay hands on the sick and they shall recover.
>
> Mark 16:17-18

> Is any sick among you afflicted? Let him pray. Is any merry? Let him sing psalms. Is any sick among you? Let him call for the elders of the church; and let them pray over him, anointing him with oil in the name of the Lord: and the prayer of faith shall save the sick, and the Lord shall raise him up; and if he has committed sins, they shall be forgiven him. Confess your faults one to another, and pray one for another, that ye may be healed. The effectual fervent prayer of a righteous man availeth much.
>
> James 5:13-16

And said, if thou wilt hearken to the voice of the Lord thy God, and wilt do that which is right in his sight, and wilt give ear to his commandments, and keep all his statutes., I will put none of these diseases upon thee, which I brought upon the Egyptians: for I am the Lord that healeth thee.
Exodus 15:26

And ye shall serve the Lord your God, and he shall bless thy bread, and thy water, and I will take sickness away from the midst of thee. There shall nothing cast their young, nor be barren in thy land: the number of thy days I will fulfill.
Exodus 23:25-26

God is looking for a vessel so that the healing power of Jesus will flow through to heal the physical man of all infirmities. The great Lawgiver said sickness is a curse.

Then the Lord will make thy plagues wonderful and the plagues of thy seed, even great plagues, and of long continuance, and sore sicknesses, and of long continuance. Moreover, he will bring upon thee all the diseases of Egypt which thou was afraid of; and they shall cleave unto thee. Also every sickness, and every plague, which is written in the book of this law, them will the Lord bring upon thee, until thou be destroyed.
Deuteronomy 28:59-61

Oh, how sweet to rest in the arms of Jesus, safe and secure from all harm. Blessed be His name, as children of the Most High God, we are redeemed from the curse of the law.

Christ hath redeemed us from the curse of the law, being made a curse for us; for it is written, curse is everyone that hangeth on a tree.
Galatians 3:13

Our bodies are the temples of the Holy Spirit.

What? Know ye not that your body is the temple of The Holy Ghost which is in you, which ye have of God, and ye are not your own. For ye are bought with a price: therefore glorify God in your body and in your spirit, which are God's.
1 Corinthians 6:19-20

For as much as ye know that ye were not redeemed with corruptible things, as silver and gold, from your vain conversation, received by tradition from your fathers; but with precious blood of Christ, as of a lamb without blemish and without spot.
1 Peter 1:18-19

Let us therefore glorify God in our bodies and in our spirits, which are God's.

There are some people who believe that physical illness is a direct result of demonic infestation and that the only route to healing is through deliverance. There are others who believe that Christians cannot be touched by demons.

Many quote scriptures as follows: "The Lord will give His angels charge over thee; the evil one shall not come nigh thy dwelling place." But let's not be narrow in our understanding of the Word of God. Search the Word diligently. There are words there to open the eyes of our understanding. For example, Matthew 10:28: "And fear not them which kill the body, but are not able to kill the soul, but rather fear Him which is able to destroy both soul and body in hell."

The devil does have power, as he did with Job, to bring disease upon a Christian but God will only allow this for his purpose. What kind of disease did Job have? Job 2 tells us that Satan afflicted Job with sores from the soles of his feet to the top of his head.

When I lie down, I say when shall I arise, and the night be gone? And I am full of tossing to and fro unto the dawning of the day. My flesh is clothed with worms and clods of dust and my skin is broken, and become loathsome.
Job 7:4-5

We are not certain what ailment Job had, but some of his symptoms throughout the book of Job suggest a combination of physical problems as follows:

> Disfigurement – "And when they lifted up their eyes afar off, and knew him not, they lifted up their voice and wept; and they rent everyone his mantle, and sprinkled dust upon their heads towards heaven." (Job 2:12)
> Parasites and Skin Infections – "My flesh is clothed with worms and clods of dust; my skin is broken and become loathsome." (Job 7:5)
> Hallucinations – "Then thou scared me with dreams, and terrifieth me through visions." (Job 7:14)
> Emaciation – "My bone cleaved to my skin and to my flesh, and I am escaped with the skin of my teeth." (Job 19:20)
> Sharp pains – "My bones are pierced in me in the night season: and my sinews take no rest." (Job 30:17)
> Fever – "My skin is black upon me, and my bones are burned with heat." (Job 30:30)

Job's sores may have been boils, painful bacterial infections of the skin. Whatever they were, this great man of God was perfect and upright. He feared God and shunned evil yet the enemy afflicted him with disease and destroyed his family and possessions. Take a look at the Apostle Paul's writing regarding affliction permitted by God.

> And lest I be exalted above measure through the abundance of the revelations, there was given to me a thorn in the flesh, the messenger of Satan to buffet me, lest I should be exalted above measure.
> For this I besought the Lord thrice, that it might depart from me. And he said unto me. My grace is sufficient for thee: for my strength is made perfect in weakness. Most gladly therefore will I rather glory in my infirmities, that the power of Christ may rest on me. Therefore I take pleasure in infirmities, in reproaches, in necessities, in persecutions, in

distresses for Christ's sake: for when I am weak, then am I strong.

2Corinthians 12:7-10

Let's aim for a demonstration of the Spirit and power of God. It was the dynamic Apostle Paul who said in the book of 1 Corinthians 2:4; and my speech and my preaching was not with enticing words of man's wisdom, but in a demonstration of the Spirit and of power. The Anointed One and His anointing abides in us therefore with confidence, we know that we are equipped and prepared to rebuke, renounce and destroy all the strongholds of the devil. If ye abide in me and my words abide in you, ye shall ask what ye will, and it shall be done unto you.

Jesus the God-man accomplished much for us on the cross, therefore through Him we are complete and we can use the power in His name to defeat the enemy even if he wages warfare against us. We must prevail, for we are not victims but victors.

Jesus declared on the cross before he gave up the ghost that it is finished. It is finished the battle is over! It is finished and there be no more war. It is finished the end of the conflict. It is finished and Jesus is Lord. Glory be to God! What a lovely and precious name, the righteous run into Him and are safe.

There is no other name under heaven given among men whereby we must be saved. Every knee must bow and every tongue confess that Jesus is Lord in heaven, in the earth and under the earth.

In the book of Luke, this great physician shows us differences in the areas of illness.

And he (Jesus) came down with them, and stood in the plain, and the company of his disciples, and a great multitude of people out of all Judea and Jerusalem, and from the sea coast of Tyre and Sidon, which came to hear, and to be healed of their diseases, and they that were vexed with unclean spirits: and they were healed.

Luke 6:17-18

It's evident that some of the diseases or illnesses were healed, and some were healed as a result of unclean spirits being cast out.

> And in the same hour he (Jesus) cured many of their infirmities and plagues, and of evil spirits; and unto many that were blind he gave sight.
>
> Luke 7:21

If we carefully search the Word we will find answers to many things that baffle the mind. Some diseases are purely physical or natural, maybe a malfunctioning of organs or systems due to deficiency of nutritious food. Some diseases are also caused by demons. I suffer from what seemed to be elephantiasis, some have cancer or various skin infections for which a proper diagnosis cannot be made.

> And as He (Jesus) was yet a-coming, the devil threw him down, and tare him. And Jesus rebuked the unclean spirit, and healed the child, and delivered him again to his father.
>
> Luke 9:42

Last but certainly not least, let's look at another account of Jesus healing.

> And in the synagogue there was a man, which had a spirit of an unclean devil, and cried out with a loud voice, saying, let us alone; what have we to do with thee, thou Jesus of Nazareth? Art thou come to destroy us? I know thee who thou are, the holy one of God. And Jesus rebuked him, saying, hold thy peace and come out of him and when the devil had thrown him in the midst, he came out of him, and hurt him not.
>
> Luke 4:33-35

The Word of the Lord says we are to search the scriptures for they testify to Jesus' life. How He approached and handled matters naturally and supernaturally will most definitely assist us on our Christian pilgrimage.

Jesus healed by rebuking evil spirits. If we therefore apply His methods, we will behold great victory over the power of darkness. We must exercise our right and say as Jesus said, "All power is given unto me." We are partakers of this divine power that pertains unto life and godliness.

Demons must subject themselves to the Christian as he or she submits to God. They must tremble and flee at the all-powerful name of Jesus.

Demons are capable of afflicting the physical body of human beings with pain. At times there can be excruciating pain in different areas or organs or systems of the body when no known diagnosis is made; this can be devastating.

The fact that damage can be done to systems or organs, yet nothing can be proven medically, is enough evidence to look to the hills wholeheartedly. Christians and non-Christians accept doctors' diagnosis and at times feel that if the doctors themselves don't know what is wrong, then what can they the patients do?

Let's not be discouraged. Take the case to the omniscient One, the ultimate judge. Allow His eyes to penetrate the darkness, the hidden and subtle craftiness of this diabolical enemy. He's the discerner of all things; He's capable of revealing things to us that we couldn't have figured out naturally.

May the eyes of our understanding be enlightened to things that can overtake a child of God if he or she is ignorant of the devil's wiles. We can be destroyed because of a lack of knowledge. We need to know when we are affected naturally and spiritually.

God promised His chosen people, the Israelites, that He wouldn't allow any of the diseases that afflicted the Egyptians to come upon them. We are His chosen generation, a royal priesthood, a holy nation, a peculiar people. Jesus' desire is for us to show forth His praises to Him continually. He brought us out of darkness into His marvelous light.

I thank God for the light. Jesus is the light of our salvation; whom shall we fear? Jesus, our great High Priest, came to the world to set the captives free and to destroy the works of the devil. Let's place Him at the highest place, far above all else, then humble ourselves and worship at His feet.

It's of great importance for Christians to distinguish between the diseased and the demonic. Now we can see quite clearly why the gift of discernment should be effective in our lives. It is only the Holy Spirit who can impart to us a real understanding of the plight of those who turn to us for help. It's only the Holy Spirit who can prevent us from saying things and acting in a way that may not only be incorrect but also harmful.

Is there any coincidence between the symptoms of demonic subjection and possession? There are similarities, and because of this, great damage has been done to people who are looking for help. Here's a typical example of a man with a mental disorder with signs and symptoms to suggest that he may have been demon-possessed or subjected.

One beautiful Sunday morning a man came to church worshipping the Lord as if it was the last breath he had in his body; therefore he was going to give all to Jesus, or so I thought. He was so excited about the Lord he couldn't help but approach everyone to let them know.

I could see that he loved the Lord very much but I discovered that he was mentally ill. You didn't have to have the gift of discernment to figure it all out. He didn't worship his Father as we did. He was much louder and he jumped up and down and threw his handkerchief up in the air, praising God joyfully. He occasionally turned to his neighbor and said, "I'm excited for Jesus."

Many people were disturbed by him and they frowned and exclaimed that he was disrupting the service. Some said he was demon possessed and began to rebuke and cast out demons. He was grabbed by the collar of his shirt, told that this spirit was not of God and ejected from the service, much to my dismay.

It's about time the church comes to the realization that we ought always to be gentle and temperate. Know who you are addressing for we are not fighting against flesh and blood but against principalities, powers, rulers of darkness and spiritual wickedness in high places.

Let's be careful that we do not exert bodily harm. Jesus never did, therefore we need to follow His example. We need to be at that place in the Lord where the Holy Spirit will surely speak to us and direct us accordingly. The Spirit of God is omniscient and intelligent. He's capable of revealing things to us.

Therefore, we needn't act as ignorant or insensitive people but instead behave as people who are led by the Holy Spirit. Take heed to the Word of God and let us heap coals upon their heads. Many people are bound by the forces of hell and they come to the hall of liberty, the place of prayer to be delivered but they are at times cast out

They could have taken their refuge among the tombstones where there is no help. This is place of doom and gloom where their situations get worst and sometimes it is hopeless and they die. Those in bondage are deprived of their natural abilities already. Let's not make it worse for them. These less fortunate people need abundant love and pleasant words.

> Pleasant words are as an honeycomb, sweet to the soul, and health to the bones.
>
> Proverbs 16:24

We need to accommodate less fortunate people. They could be among the tombs like the madman of Gadara, mean and fierce. Some are sleeping on the streets and some are eating out of the garbage bins, but when they enter the house of prayer, pray, saints in Christ, for the mentally ill and the prayer of faith will heal the sick.

This is the place where lives are changed, burdens are lifted, the yokes are destroyed, the lame must walk, the blind must see and all fetters are broken. Our God can do exceedingly more than we can imagine or think.

Those who are captive may not wear Estee Lauder or Boss cologne or perfume but let's put our arms around them and embrace them. Jesus helped them. He was not scornful of anyone.

The Word of the Lord declares that God anointed Jesus of Nazareth with the Holy Ghost and with power, and He went about doing good and healing all that were oppressed of the devil, for God was with Him.

May we be anointed like He was so that when we see those who are regressed, repressed, suppressed, depressed, obsessed, oppressed and possessed we can say with authority, "The Spirit of the Lord God is upon me to loose those that are bound by the enemy. He has anointed me to set the captive free and whom Jesus sets free is free indeed. Glory be to God."

CHAPTER 12

Are We Ready?

It's sad to say that many people are lost in a world of gloom and darkness bound by Satan and his demons. They live a life of misery and hopelessness. What will become of these people? Some have died without help and many walk the roads of life just looking on. This is where the church, and Christ Jesus the Head of the church, should and must step in to help.

But is the church ready for such combat? The church is commissioned to cast out devils and therefore men and women of courage should set out to bring freedom to those who are regressed, repressed, suppressed, depressed, oppressed, obsessed or even possessed by the devil's power.

It's time for the church to arise and come to the realization that Satan has his church and that church is growing in unity and power. What about the church of the living God? Some are divided to the very core. It's time for the church to take a righteous and steadfast stand together looking unto Him who is able to keep us from falling.

The apostle Paul wrote about the carnal man.

> For ye are yet carnal: For whereas there is among you envying, and strife and divisions, are ye not carnal, and walk as men?
> 1 Corinthians 3:3

God is calling for His church to be in unity.

Behold, how good and how pleasant it is for brethren to dwell together in unity. It is like the precious ointment upon the head, that runs down upon the beard, even Aaron's beard: that went down to the skirts of his garments; As the dew of Hermon, and as the dew that descended upon the mountains of Zion: For there the Lord commanded the blessing, even life for evermore.

Psalm 133:1-3

Let's try to keep the unity of the Spirit in the bond of peace.

Endeavoring to keep the unity of the spirit in the bond of peace.

Ephesians 4:3

Till we all come in the unity of the faith, and of the knowledge of the Son of God, unto a perfect man, unto the measure of the stature of the fullness of Christ.

Ephesians 4:13

The Bible tells us that every kingdom divided against itself will be ruined and every city or household divided against itself will not stand. In the book of Matthew 12:25; Jesus addressed the Pharisees, He said, every kingdom divided against itself is brought to desolation; and every city or house divided against itself shall not stand.

Are the members of the church (the body of Christ) the blood-bought saints, to learn from the devil and his organization? I don't think so! The church is the bride of Christ and we are admonished to be an example of the believers, in word, in conversation, in charity, in spirit, in faith and purity.

The church is empowered to impact its people of all nationalities; therefore we must be a witness to the world. The first century church was not a defeated church; they cast out devils everywhere they went. Their spiritual antennas were functioning, they could not be deceived.

In Satan's church weaklings or traitors are not supported but destroyed; a person has to be alert and strong to survive in the coven. The church must be strong in the Lord and in the power of His might. Be watchful and ready always to tread upon the lion and the adder.

The Young lion and the dragon we must trample under our feet in the name of Jesus Christ of Nazareth. This is the word of Jesus to His disciples in Luke 10:19; behold, I give you power to tread on serpents and scorpions, and over all the power of the enemy: and nothing shall by any means hurt you.

The church is fragmented and this has given the devil a foothold or doorway to gain access and create havoc in the body of Christ. War, strife, friction, sexual immorality, malice, theft, slander, gossip, and witchcraft are rampant in the church. Each member should walk one with another in love. We ought to love our neighbor as ourselves.

Physical maladies, misfortune, financial problems, accidents, stagnation, complacency and lethargy are some of the obstacles facing the church. Satan and his demons have entered in by the doorway and are making a mockery of the church.

It's time for the church to sound the alarm and wake us all up. Those who are of the day cannot be found sleeping. The Word of the Lord says we are to watch and pray lest we fall into temptation. Matthew 26:41; watch and pray that ye enter not into temptation: the spirit indeed is willing, but the flesh is weak.

Learning from Witches?

Witches come together to give homage to their master, while members of the church gather together to worship our God and King. Does the church worship Him with the kind of reverence shown by the witches toward Satan?

If the church will not take on the responsibility of the church, then let's take a lesson from Satan's ministers or demons. When the witches come together to worship there are 13 of them together with 13 candles in a circle. They do everything in unison.

They dress identically in long white robes with attached cowl-like hoods up over their heads. They each sit cross-legged on the floor, back straight, arms folded across their breasts, staring with absolute concentration into the candles in front of them.

These witches do not wear jewelry or ornamentation of any sort. There is no movement by any of them except for their continuous low-voiced chanting and humming as they offer their prayers to Satan.

These ministers of darkness have a very consistent prayer life. They pray for fame, power and the destruction of God's church. It is not their delight for the church to be uplifted by the Spirit of God from glory to glory. They are aware of the fact that light will shine in darkness and will expose and defeat them.

Nora, a witch and one of Satan's personal brides, was told that if she wanted anything all she needed to do was to light a candle and put her prayers underneath it. Requests for others should be included. She was told she could pray for another person's uplifting or his downfall.

It is absolutely no time to play church, it is imperative that we know who we are in Christ and be cognizant of the fact that Devil and his cohorts are praying for our downfall and destruction. Let's praise the Lord for Jesus Christ of Nazareth who is resurrected and is at the right hand of God praying for you and me. Do these disciples of Satan achieve much through their prayers? Yes, they do! Let's be careful to observe how well co-coordinated and unified they are. They have an understanding of the importance of order in their organization.

Note well, there is absolutely no bickering, whispering or complaining during their time of worship. They dress appropriately and they move their bodies in one accord. Their undivided attention is given to their master as they enter the inner courts of hell to make their requests known. One of their prayers is for people to be enslaved by them through depression, oppression, possession and so forth.

Isn't it evident in the church that there are many foul or unclean spirits manifesting? They utter or mutter their evil incantation against individuals and churches. After a while the church's prayer base is destroyed.

What is incantation? It is a formula, or charm words, used to produce magical or supernatural effects. We often quote the scripture that the gates of hell shall not prevail against the church of the living God. The gates of hell can, however, prevail if the church is not found praying fervently and persistently until God's glory comes down.

The Word of the Lord tells us first that we should offer requests for all of mankind and then to pray for all saints.

> I exhort therefore, that first of all, supplications, prayers, intercessions, and giving of thanks, be made for all men. For kings, and for all that are in authority; that we may lead a quiet and peaceable life in all goodness and honesty. For this is good and acceptable in the sight of God our savior; who will have all men to be saved, and to come unto the knowledge of the truth.
> 1 Timothy 2:1-4.

> Praying always with all prayer and supplication in the spirit, and watching thereunto with all perseverance and supplication for all saints.
> Ephesians 6:18

The enemy has ravaged the church for too long. From the days of John the Baptist the church suffereth violence and violence take it by force. Jesus said to the Apostle Peter in the book of Matthew chapter 16:18; and I say also unto thee, that thou art Peter, and upon this rock I will build my church: and the gates of hell shall not prevail against it. It's time to take back what the enemy has stolen. As Christ gave Himself for the church because He loved it, we also need to devote ourselves to the service of the Lord.

> That he might present it to himself, a glorious church, not having spot, or wrinkle, or any such thing; But that it should be holy and without blemish.
> Ephesians 5:27

Therefore, let's watch and pray, be alert and vigilant for the adversary is like a roaring lion seeking to destroy the body of Christ. However, no weapon formed against God's people will prosper. Let's begin to saturate ourselves in prayer concerning our leaders, brothers, sisters and everything pertaining to the church. Let's show the devil that if his followers can come together, then we can do likewise as prescribed in God's Word.

> Blow the trumpet in Zion, sanctify a fast, call a solemn assembly: gather the people, sanctify the congregation, assemble the elders, gather the children, and those that suck the breast: let the bridegroom go forth of his chamber, and the bride out of her closet. Let the priests, the ministers of the Lord, weep between the porch and the altar, and let them say, spare my people, O Lord, and give not thane heritage to reproach, that the heathen should rule over them: wherefore should they say among the people, where is their god. Then will the Lord be jealous for his land, and pity his people.
> Joel 2:15-18

God's jealousy is an expression of His deep love for, and commitment to, His people. Only after all of God's people are gathered together and cry out to Him as one will the Lord be jealous for His people and pity them. Church, let's fast and pray until God releases His explosive power to destroy, tear down and pull down the strongholds of the enemy.

Let us bear this in our minds, that the blood-bought church of the living God of which we are a part is armed and extremely dangerous. We are to dress like soldiers, from our heads to our feet. Remember the armor in the book of Ephesians chapter 6:11-17; you have the double edged sword in your hand and in your mouth and it is your weapon to cut down or bring to nought the plots of the enemy.

In Romans 10: 8; the Word of the Lord says, that the Word is nigh us, even in our mouth and in our heart is the word of faith, which we preach.

The Word is also in the mind and the heart and this Word is like a hammer, it breaks a rock to pieces and it is like fire, it burns.

The Word of the Lord declares in 1 Corinthians 10:13 there hath no temptation taken you but such as is common to man: but God is faithful, who will not suffer you to be tempted above that you are able; but will with the temptation also make a way of escape, that you may be able to bear it.

Epilogue

I should have died back in Jamaica, given the demonic forces that were unleashed against me through witches and wizards. But God spared my life because He has a better plan for me. Praise God, from whom all blessings flow, I don't have to take refuge under the shadow of Satan's mighty power.

They do not have to bathe me in oil; neither do I have to walk around with a jazy fragrance that's offensive to the human race.

What is the significance of wearing guard rings or throwing rice and eggs before retiring for bed? All this nonsense is rendered ineffective under the incorruptible blood of Jesus Christ. The life of the flesh is in the blood of Jesus Christ of Nazareth.

I like this verse of scripture in Leviticus 17:11: "for the life of the flesh is in the blood and I have given it upon the altar to make atonement for your souls: for it is the blood that makes atonement for the soul."

O, I thank God for the gift of salvation for my life. As a result of Jesus' journey of sufferings to the finish line, I am part-taker of His divine power. The blood flowing from His scourged back, His bruised head, His pierced hands, feet and side was life for me. This blood by faith in Jesus Christ of Nazareth is all over and it is keeping me alive.

My mother's efforts couldn't spare me. Her prayers carried me for a while, then God desired that I seek a relationship with Him because I was at the age of accountability and He wanted to save me and take me down to the potter's house to fashion me for His perfect plan.

I hadn't succumbed to the plan initially but thank God in time I learned from what was written about the rebellious Israelites who over and over again had to be reminded of God's power and grace.

I give homage to my God who is supreme, all-powerful, all-wise and everywhere present, and the creator of all things. I give Him thanks for relationship with Him through His Son Jesus Christ. I have dominion over Satan and his power and I live a victorious life above and beyond fear and phobias, superstition and evil curses.

The greater One is living within me. The Word of the Lord says, "ye are of God little children, and have overcome them: because greater is He that is in you than he that is in the world." 1 John 4:4; says, ye are of God, little children, and have overcome them: because greater is he that is in you, than ye that is in the world.

I'm a conqueror, I'm victorious, and I'm reigning with Jesus. I'm seated in heavenly places with Him for the kingdom of God is within me. Yes! In all these things I am more than a conqueror through Jesus who loved me and gave his life for me.

To God be the glory, the honor and praise for sending Jesus to redeem me from the curse of the law. I must laud His name. It is above every other name. Every knee shall bow and every tongue confess that Jesus Christ is Lord.

Yes, Jesus is Lord in the heavens, in the earth and under the earth, the head of all principalities and powers of darkness and we are complete in Him. Thank God that Jesus overcame the enemy on the cross, spoiling all principalities, making a public spectacle of them. Jesus the great High Priest has power and authority. He has the power over the devil and his demons. Devil, you're a defeated foe.

> He made that declaration when he said, all power is given unto me in heaven and in the earth.
> Matthew 28:18

> He that committeth sin is of the devil; for the devil sinneth from the beginning. For this purpose the son of God was manifested, that he might destroy the works of the devil.
> 1John 3:8

There is victory for God's people through the blood of Jesus. Scourged, pierced, broken was the body of Jesus Christ of Nazareth but the blood that flows reach the highest mountain and the lowest valley. The blood of Jesus is still effective in this dispensation of grace which is the church age.

Giving up the splendor of heaven, the glory and riches, Jesus became poor that we may be rich. What a price He paid to shed His incorruptible blood for us. Without the shedding of His blood there is no forgiveness, glory be to God.

> Who, being in the form of God, thought it not robbery to be equal with God: But made himself of no reputation, and took upon him the form of a servant, and was made in the likeness of men: and being found in fashion as a man, he humbled himself, and became obedient unto death, even the death of the cross.
>
> Philippians 2:6-8

I thank God for Jesus who willingly died for us. The shedding of His blood once and for all atones for our sin. Praise God. The holy saving blood of Jesus has power and dominion over demonic forces. Our protection is in the blood of Jesus.

Often a Christian can be heard pleading the blood of Jesus on his life, children, properties, businesses and church. Even though the expression is not scriptural, it's accepted in Zion as an expression of our faith or prayer.

When we plead the blood of Jesus, we are asking Him to be with us in His power, glory, authority and protection.

If God protected His people by the blood of unblemished lambs in the Old Testament what about the saving blood of Jesus?

When God intended to destroy all the first-born sons of the Egyptians, the Israelites were told to kill a year-old lamb and sprinkle its blood with bunches of hyssop on the two side posts and lintel of the door of their houses. When the death angel passed through Egypt on that fateful night and saw the blood on the door posts he spared the first-born within.

Oh what a protection then, but now Jesus' blood is on our souls. The blood of Jesus ransomed His people and we can rest assured, and very secure in His love, knowing His blood is on our souls. We can spread the word that the blood of Jesus is all over us and it's keeping us alive. Yes, it builds a defense against Satan and his demons. Let's glorify Him continually because our God is worthy to be praised.

We do give God thanks for the written Word to conquer Satan and his demons. If we rightly divide this Word of truth, there will be a positive effect. The Word of God is not passive but it is active and alive, penetrating and sharper than any two edged sword.

> For the word of God is quick, and powerful, and sharper than any two-edged sword piercing even to the dividing asunder of soul and spirit, and of joints and marrow, and is a discerner of the thoughts and intents of the heart must be in our hands.
>
> Hebrews 4:12

Let's therefore heed the Word of the Lord and leave the old way of life and let us put the garment of the new man. Let's hunger and thirst for the Word of God because it is life unto us when lay hold of it and it is also health to our flesh.

No principality or power of darkness will conquer a child of God who is armed and dangerous and ready to say: "Thus saith the Lord," or "It is written, devil." Let us cleave to the Word. It's vital for our growth from babes to maturity. The Word of the Lord declares that we are to grow in His grace and knowledge.

> Let the word of Christ dwell in you richly in all wisdom; teaching and admonishing one another in psalms and hymns and spiritual songs, singing with grace in your hearts to the Lord.
>
> Colossians 3:16

Jesus was acquainted with the Word of God. He read from the book of the prophet Isaiah: "The spirit of the Lord is upon me; because the Lord hath anointed me to preach good tidings unto the meek; He hath sent me to bind up the broken-hearted, to proclaim liberty to the captives and the opening of the prison to them that are bound."

Jesus quoted the Word and overcame the devil by the power and authority that is in the Word. At the weakest moment of his life, having fasted for forty days and forty nights, the devil tempted Jesus. He thought he would be victorious over Him when Jesus, in the form of man, was hungry. The devil commanded Jesus to make bread of stones. Jesus responded that man does not live by bread alone, but by every word that proceedeth out of the mouth of God. Satan is defeated. Hallelujah!

Satan doesn't give up easily. He will try anything or everything to trap you. He took Jesus up on a pinnacle of the temple and said unto Him: "If thou be the son of God, cast thyself down." The devil knew the Word of God, having dwelt with Him at one time. The Word of the Lord says that the devil was full of wisdom, and perfect beauty even to the point of quoting scripture to Jesus.

> "For he will give his angels charge over thee, to keep thee in all thy ways, they shall bear thee up in their hands, lest thou dash thy foot against a stone.
> Psalm 91:11-12

Then Jesus defeated the devil again by saying: "It is written, thou shalt not tempt the Lord thy God." Undefeated, the devil thought by now Jesus would be weary and would succumb to his temptations.

This constantly defeated foe took Jesus onto an exceedingly high mountain and showed Him all the kingdoms of the world and their glory then said to Him, "All these things will I give you, if thou wilt fall down and worship me."

We are aware of the fact that God anointed Jesus of Nazareth with the Holy Ghost and power. He rebuked the devil with great authority when He said: "Get thee hence Satan. It is written, thou shalt worship the Lord thy God, and Him only shalt thou serve."

Eventually the devil had to leave Jesus alone because the Word was too fiery for him to resist. The temptations were an ordeal for Jesus because the flesh was weak. However, He resisted the devil to the very end and if we also resist him he will have to flee.

We the followers of Jesus Christ will have to fight this battle, rightly dividing the Word of God. We have to say, "It is written," open our mouths and let the Word go forth as fire. God's Word is pure Word, buried in the furnace of the earth, refined seven times.

God's Word is eternal, unchangeable and complete. It stands firm in the heavens. Let's lay hold of His Word. May God's people have a relish for His unadulterated word. Study it, memorize it, meditate on it, and let it not depart from your eyes. When the Word indwells you richly in times of need the Comforter, the Strengthener, the One who directs, speaks, leads and teaches, will withdraw from the heart and mind, then with confidence you can say, "It is written."

> "This book of the law shall not depart out of thy mouth; but thou shalt meditate therein day and night, that thou mayest observe to do according to all that is written therein: For then thou shalt make thy way prosperous, and then shalt thou have good success.
>
> Joshua 1:8

> Study to show thyself approved unto God, a workman that needeth not to be ashamed, rightly dividing the word of truth.
>
> 2 Timothy 2:15

There is great dominion in the Word of God and this is found in the Bible, the book of books, the only living book known to man to preserve itself with great power. The Bible is to be treasured. It has unique authority over all books. God has invested dominion in His inspired, written Word.

> All scripture is given by inspiration of God, and is profitable for doctrine, for reproof, for correction, for instruction in righteousness: That the man of God may be perfect, thoroughly furnished completely unto all good works.
>
> 2 Timothy 3:16-17

Lord, prepare us to be a vessel or sanctuary, pure and holy, tried and true, to be thoroughly furnished completely unto all good works—and to rebuke, renounce and smash to pieces all the plans or works of the devil. The Word of God says all power is given unto us.

> And Jesus came and spake unto them, saying, all power is given unto me in heaven and in earth.
> Matthew 28:18

We have an Anchor that keeps the soul steadfast and sure while the billows roll, fastened to the rock which cannot move, grounded firm and deep in the Savior's love. Lay hold of this precious Word in the book of Hebrew 6:19, "which hope we have as an anchor of the soul, both sure and steadfast, and goes through the curtain of the heavenly temple into the inner sanctuary.

Our God is a consuming fire." The fire of God has an effect on those He touches. He's so faithful, thank God; He's involved in every detail of our lives. What He says He will do, for His word stand firm in the heavens. He will stand by or hasten His Word to perform it. God promised His chosen people that He wouldn't allow them to be defeated.

Jesus became curse for us all that we may the righteousness of God. For we know the grace of our Lord Jesus Christ, that He was rich, yet for our sakes He became poor, in order to make you rich by means of His poverty.

The devil, the enemy of our soul, is a defeated foe. It doesn't matter how contentious or presumptuous he might be, though he rages we shall not be defeated. Jesus, after providing purification for our sins, sat at the right hand of majesty. He has spoiled all principalities and power and made a show of them openly and triumphed over them in Himself.

We are the blood-bought church of the living God. Jesus' life was poured out for our protection.

> For the life of the flesh is in the blood: And I have given it to you upon the altar to make atonement for your souls: for it is the blood that maketh atonement for the soul.
>
> Leviticus 17:11

We must know in whom we have believed. Let's take a stand with Him in the heavenlies, knowing without wavering that all wicked spirits and Satan are under our feet. We need to declare and decree that Satan and his wicked spirits are subject to us in the name of Jesus Christ.

Onward Christian soldiers, marching as to war, let's stand and having done all to stand, stand in the victory of the ascension and the glorification of our precious Lord Jesus Christ, whereby all the principalities and powers are made subject to Him. Glory be to God! He's worthy to be praised.

Colossians 2:10 tells us we are complete in Him, which is the Head of all principalities and power. We do give God thanks for the spiritual armor that's available to His children.

Will we take time out and dress for war and like David refused to dress in Saul's armor, but instead put on the armor of God, the One who never lost a battle? Thank God He's the great King of Glory, strong and mighty. Glory be to God, He is mighty in battle. Who can contend with God's power? Power and might are within His hand. No one can withstand Him. He's God and God alone.

Let's dress up, church, in the girdle of truth, the breastplate of righteousness, the sandals of peace, and the helmet of salvation. Are you ready for war? Fight like a soldier and be alert and watchful.

Lift up the shield of faith against all the fiery darts of the enemy. Hold the sword of the Spirit in your hands. He teaches our hands to war so that a bow of steel is broken by our arms. Use the Word of God against all the forces of the enemy. Never cease to encourage yourself with the Word of God.

> For the weapons of our warfare are not carnal, but mighty through God to the pulling down of strongholds; casting down imaginations and every high thing that exalteth itself

against the knowledge of God, and bringing into captivity every thought to the obedience of Christ.
1 Corinthians 10:4-5

Though I walk in the midst of trouble, Thou wilt revive me. Thou shalt stretch forth thine hand against the wrath of mine enemies, and thy right hand shall save me. The Lord will perfect that which concerneth me: Thy mercy, O Lord, endureth forever: Forsake not the works of thine own hands.
Psalm 138:7-8

Thank God for victory!

References

Demons the answer book by Lester Sumrall.

Occult bondage and deliverance- Kurt. E. Koch.

Witchcraft in the pews- George Bloomer.

He came to set the captive free- Doctor Rebecca Brown

Endorsements

The Bible cautions us that we should not be ignorant concerning the devices and strategies of Satan and his demonic activities, which is so evident in our world and communities. "Lest Satan should get an advantage of us: for we are not ignorant of his devices." (2 Cor 2:11. KJV)

Rev. Joy Vassal's book "Demons are Real" is a rear accomplishment. Her dedicated effort and life experience and most importantly the Scriptural foundation upon which she approaches the subject is indeed inspirational, enlightening, and easy to read. This book ought to find its place in the hands and collection of all who seeks to be spiritually equipped for spiritual warfare against Demonic activities.

Doctor Bishop Huel Wilson
Senior Pastor/West Toronto New Testament Church of God

The Rev. Joy Vassal has been an intercessor, a prayer warrior, an inspiration, and a source of encouragement in my life. I commend her for the bold step in sharing her testimony revealing the fact that "Demons Are Real." I believe this is just a chapter of the life of this extraordinary woman of God. Certainly an eye opener to many and a reminder to some that the devil and his demons are busy at work. This book will provide you with tools to help you live victoriously in this demonic age.

Marvia Providence
Evangelist/ International Gospel Artist

Demons Are Real

This book is a real expository work on the hidden truth about demons and their operations on earth. Ministers are often very reluctant to teach or talk about demons, the result is that we have left the church vulnerable to destruction. Rev. Joy Vassal has written a complete book, starting from her encounter with the demonic and ending in divine revelation on how to defeat the demons in our life, all inspired by the Holy Spirit.

Demons Are Real is a must for every Christian home and church study groups as it can be used as a reference book in the study of demons.

We have many Christian books in the bookstores but not many share a real life experience like this one.

Rev. Don Ifepe/ Publisher Miles Magazine

This book deals with a topic that is scarcely covered in our day- Demonology. The Reverend Joy Vassal shares her traumatic story, one where Satan unleashed a host of his demons to destroy her life. It is a story of victory!

Demons are Real provides helpful insight in how to overcome the powers of darkness. This book will serve to inform believers and make them aware of Satan's cunning devices. It's a good addition to one's library!

Andrew Binda, Administrative Bishop
Church of God in Eastern Canada

Rev. Joy Vassal has meticulously exposed the powers of darkness that defeats the plan of Satan and has revealed the strategy to live a victorious live in Christ. The author has brought a new light on Ephesians 6:12; which states "For we wrestle not against flesh and blood, but against principalities, against powers, against the rulers of the darkness of this world, against spiritual wickedness in high places." It is with pleasure that I recommend your book as a must read for those who intend to live victoriously in the 21st Century.

    Reverend Sanneth Brown
    The New Testament Church of Christ the Redeemer of Canada

CPSIA information can be obtained at www.ICGtesting.com
Printed in the USA
LVOW041317270112

265811LV00002B/200/A